This study
belongs to

A FIVE-WEEK BIBLE STUDY
FASHIONED FOR GOD'S DAUGHTERS.

The

ABCs

of

GOD'S
PROMISES

*Learn to take hold of God's truth for
your life and live in triumph.*

HEATHER STAHLMAN

CONTENTS

A NOTE FROM THE AUTHOR

The ABCs of God's Promises was written as Jesus taught me to accept nothing but His truth for my life. While I was on the way home from a conference that had affirmed specific promises the Lord had spoken to me, the liar, Satan himself, tried to convince me of who I was not. It was then that Jesus' promises that had been written on the tablet of my heart started shouting! I could no longer accept the lies of the enemy, but rather, I had to proclaim the promises of God for my life. The Holy Spirit reminded me who God said I was, starting with "A" and going all the way to "Z". I heard the words my Father in heaven spoke over me before the foundations of the earth were laid, and He prompted me to find and write the actual promises from His living Word. I used the New International Version of the Holy Bible while writing this Bible study. I pray this book helps you to receive the promises of God in a personal and profound way.

Heather

ABOUT THE AUTHOR

Heather Stahlman is a lover and passionate follower of Jesus Christ. She is a blessed wife, mother of three lovely daughters, teacher of the Living Word, author and speaker. Heather was born and raised in Lewisville, TX. Heather graduated from the University of North Texas with a Bachelor of Arts in Political Science and a Minor in Spanish. She then earned a teaching certificate and taught high school Spanish until she became a mother.

Heather was a leader and facilitator of a women's Bible study for three years and now helps facilitate women's ministry events. Heather continues to teach and encourage groups of women, small and large, who desire to know Jesus in a more intimate way. By Jesus' grace, *The ABCs of God's Promises* is her first authored and published Bible study.

When Heather isn't writing she enjoys family time at their working ranch in West Texas, playing Phase 10, and hosting dinners and potlucks.

TIPS FOR SUCCESS

I am so glad that you have made the decision to complete this Bible study!
In Matthew 24:35, Jesus said, "Heaven and earth will pass away, but my words
will never pass away." As we study God's Word, we are building our foundation
on the rock of Christ which will prove unshakable when faced with the
storms of life!

Things You Should Know Before We Begin:

1. Bible Version

Use the New International Version of the Bible as you complete the lessons each week.
This is the version I used while writing the study. Of course, you can use another
version, but know that the questions will not be as clear if you do.

2. Small Groups

This study is designed for small group participation. Grab a few friends and set
a specific day of the week to unite and discuss each week together. The scripture,
questions, and reading lend for great discussion and revelations from the Holy Spirit.
You can do the study solo, but it is more powerful when you are connected
in community. You will find the answers in the back for extra guidance.

3. Weekly Lessons

Each weekly lesson is divided into five daily parts. For example: Day 1, Day 2, etc.
Set a specific time and day to start each week, and complete one day at a time.
You may do more than one day in a particular sitting, but you will benefit most
by soaking in the designated lessons individually.

4. Verse Citation

At places in the study you will see a verse cited that involves a lowercase letter (for example, Isaiah 40:31a). This is a means of breaking down each verse. Isaiah 40:31a focuses only on the first part of the verse, Isaiah 40:31b focuses on the middle, and Isaiah 40:31c focuses on the end. This format is not used in every Bible. Some will have it and some will not.

5. ♥ Heart Graphic

The heart graphic indicates a personal question that you do not have to answer in front of the small group. These are intended to make you think and enable you to be as honest as you can. I hope they will bring new insight into your walk with the Lord. If you want to share what the Lord is doing in your life, it is encouraged and welcomed.

6. Challenge Questions

At times Challenge Questions may be presented. These are for the students who like more challenge in their study. You may need a commentary to answer these questions.

7. Persevere

God has many amazing promises in His word. I pray your soul is strengthened and encouraged as we seek the Lord together. If you happen to fall behind in the study, do not be discouraged. Pick right back up where you left off and ask the Lord for His strength and discipline to know Him. He is an ever-present help!

ACKNOWLEDGEMENTS

Thank You, God, for completing this good work in me that You started and brought to completion through Jesus! Thank You for Your wisdom, understanding, and revelation through Your Holy Spirit! Thank You for orchestrating this wonderful task with Your handpicked team.

Pastor Mike and Denise, you two are wonderful shepherds, and I appreciate your godly wisdom and love.

Jenny, your God-given talent for design and craftsmanship is breathtaking. Thank you for taking chances, doing new things, and demonstrating His steadfastness!

Joanne, your edits and suggestions added to the beauty of this book. Thank you for showing me what endurance looks like.

Sarah, thank you for fanning the flame on the gift of God which is in me! You helped me embrace the gift of writing and teaching, and I am so thankful.

Matthew and Kathryn, your encouragement helped make this project a reality.

Focus group, thank you for opening your hearts to what Jesus has shared with me. Your input and vulnerability made this work complete.

And Rob, thank you for always being a shield around me.

Millie, Leni, and Trinity–
May you always walk in the fear of the Lord.
Jesus loves you, and I love you.

Mom

WEEK

One

Day 1

So is my word that goes out from my mouth: it will not return to me empty,

but will accomplish what I desire and achieve the purpose for which I sent it.

Isaiah 55:11

𝒜. Adored—loved and respected (someone) deeply.[1]

It is only appropriate to start from the beginning of the English alphabet. The Lord knows words are very important to me. After all, He is the One who knit this intricate detail into my heart. So, in writing The ABCs of God's Promises, God knew I needed His affirmations from A, all the way to Z. He didn't want any room left for me to think that something was missing. The Beginning and the End Himself, He filled in all the gaps. So, let's get started. We are going to explore God's truth and promises for His adored children.

I love Isaiah. A dear friend of mine knows how very much I love this book of the Bible! In fact, it was a running joke that I would read Isaiah anytime, anywhere. I gave a speech at my husband's thirty-fourth birthday and as I hit the glass with my fork to capture everyone's attention, she expected nothing less than a chapter from Isaiah! I did not quote Isaiah at his birthday party, but if I had wanted my husband to know how much God adored him in that moment, I would have!

I am reminded how much God adores me when I read the promises in Isaiah, and I know you will feel His adoration for you too. So, let's start there!
Read Isaiah 60:1-17 and answer the following questions.

1. In verse one, what are the two commands?

[1]www.lexico.com

2. According to verse one, what enables you to arise and shine?

3. In the midst of darkness covering the earth and thick darkness the peoples, what will happen concerning you? (v 2)

4. Why should you lift up your eyes and look about? (v 4)

5. What does the Lord your God, the Holy One of Israel, endow you with? (v 9)

6. Including verses 1-17, how many times do you count the words *you* and *your*?

7. What verse(s) make you feel loved and respected deeply? Why?
   (This can be found in Isaiah or any book of the Bible)

As I read verses one through four, the Lord brought this to my attention: In order for someone to be commanded to "Arise...", they had to have been down, whether emotionally or physically. And, in verse four, I picture someone looking down in order to receive the command "Lift up your eyes..." Perhaps this person is oblivious to the spiritual reality at hand. I can imagine the natural circumstance looked so grim, it was hard for them to believe the greater things promised. Knowing this, our Heavenly Father told them what to do and what reality was theirs, in spite of the thick darkness over some of the people!

As you read this prophecy given to Isaiah, you may notice that it is about Zion's glory. It is often referred to as "the city of our God" and "the city of the great King" (Psalm 48). Mount Zion is the city that God will establish forever (Psalm 48:8 NASB)[2]. Not only was this prophecy relevant for Isaiah and Israel in his time, but I believe it is even more relevant for us today.

This particular chapter in Isaiah speaks of Jesus as our Savior, Redeemer, the Mighty One of Jacob, and echoes the prophecies of the sons and daughters of God reigning victoriously in the kingdom of God to be established forever and ever (Isaiah 60:18-21, Revelation 22:5). So be encouraged; not only is this promise for Zion, but it is also for you and me and our future glory because of the finished work of the cross that Jesus won for us!

In the question section above, I had you count the number of "you" and "yours" to reiterate that this promise is for you! Forty-four times God used the word you/your in verses 1-17. I hope you understand you are His everlasting pride and joy and He adores you. Instead of bronze, He will bring you gold! To me, this means, "You are first place, not third." Jesus is your peace and well-being, and you can trust His eternal reign and leadership over your life.

[2] Compellingtruth.org/Zion.html

Then you will look and be radiant, your heart will throb
and swell with joy; the wealth on the seas will be brought to you,
to you the riches of the nations will come.
Isaiah 60:5a

Notes

_____

_____

_____

_____

_____

_____

_____

_____

_____

_____

_____

_____

_____

Day 2

I am my beloved's and my beloved is mine;
Song of Songs 6:3a

 Beloved—dearly loved.[3]

 Chosen—one who is the object of choice or of divine favor: an elect person.[4]

 Daughter—a girl or woman in relation to either or both of her parents.[5]

There is something special about being referred to as beloved. I love the song "His Banner Over Me Is Love." I especially love the verse *I'm my Beloved's and He is mine*. When I hear my heavenly Father call me beloved, I know I am dearly loved.

The thought of being *chosen* also gives me a great sense of value. To know that God has chosen me, and I did not choose Him, blows me away. The Ancient of Days and Creator of everything in heaven and on earth, chose *me*.

Let's read Colossians 3:12-15 and Ephesians 6:13-18.

1. In Colossians, what five things are God's chosen people, holy and dearly loved, supposed to clothe themselves with? (v 12)

[3] www.meriam-webster.com [4] Ibid [5] www.lexico.com

♥ Do you have a grievance with another person? If so, lift that disagreement up before the Lord. Do not let the enemy sow seeds of bitterness and rob the peace of Christ from your heart.

2. Are verses twelve and thirteen a command or a suggestion?

3. What binds these virtues together in perfect unity? (v 14)

4. Why are we to let the peace of Christ rule in our hearts? (v 15)

♥ Do you believe you can have an unthankful attitude and the peace of Christ ruling in your heart at the same time? Why, or why not?

5. According to Ephesians, we are to stand firm with what buckled around our waist? (v 14)

6. Still in verse fourteen, what type of breastplate are we to have in place?

7. How should our feet be fitted? (v 15)

8. What does the shield of faith do? (v 16)

9. How are we to pray and who are we to pray for? (v 18)

My pastor gave an encouraging and timely message in church this morning as he referenced Ephesians 6:12-18. I had been pondering Colossians 3:12-15, as I had started writing this day for the Bible study the night prior. Wow. God is always on time. I had not considered the parallels of Ephesians and Colossians.

In Colossians, the Lord commands us to clothe ourselves with the godly virtues of *compassion, kindness, humility, gentleness,* and *patience.* We don't leave our homes naked. We clothe ourselves every day. The same principal goes with each of these virtues. We are to put them on, just as we would put on our daily clothes.

He continues to instruct us to *bear with each other* and *forgive* one another if anyone has a grievance. One definition of grievance is: a real or imagined wrong or other cause for complaint or protest, especially unfair treatment. The enemy prowls around trying to offend members of the body of Christ and strip them of their godly garments with the silliest reasons.

I love verses fourteen and fifteen too. We cannot miss that LOVE binds each of these virtues together and glues the body of Christ together in peace. We are members of one body, not two or three or four.

Regarding peace, I do not believe we can have the peace of Christ in our hearts if thankfulness is absent. I can use the current situation that I am in now, to prove my point. We are currently in the process of selling our land to a developer. We have been under contract now for seventy-four days, but there is one day left that they can back out of the deal. Tomorrow, we will know if they have decided to stay in the contract they made with us, or back out with a very minor consequence. Again, I can clearly see that the enemy is trying to steal the peace of Christ from my heart, but I have chosen to thank the Lord instead.

This morning I was thanking Him, and picturing our land and all of the many blessings and memories He has given us on this particular piece of property. My thankful heart allowed the peace of Christ to reign in my heart instead of worry about what tomorrow's decision will be. I am thankful regardless, and because of that, I have the peace that Jesus Himself gives me. In Ephesians, Paul actually talks about the *gospel* of peace!

I get so excited when I see similarities and cross references between certain scriptures. When the Holy Spirit teaches me how the Word is interconnected, I feel as if I've won a huge prize. In reality, I have won! I am gaining His knowledge and wisdom and there's nothing better than heavenly treasure. So, let's explore some parallels of these two books.

Paul the Apostle wrote both books, Colossians and Ephesians, and he instructs us to put on some things. In Ephesians, we're commanded to put on armor instead of clothes. Paul had the Roman soldiers in mind concerning the armor. Generally speaking, armor is outerwear which is worn in battle and to protect our bodies and vital organs, whereas, the clothing in Colossians is put on first and imperative for use every day.

The first piece of armor that Paul mentions in Ephesians is the belt of truth. Knowing Jesus' truth allows us to stand firm so we aren't swept away by the enemy's lies. God's Word is truth and it is what the Holy Spirit reminds us of when we are in need. The Holy Spirit is our helper who guides us into all truth. Jesus also commands us to guard our hearts and our minds in Him, who is the Truth. As we read His truth, our hearts and minds are guarded and protected in Jesus. When I pray over my daughters at night, I generally ask Jesus to guard and protect my daughters' hearts and minds, and I know that He, Himself, will do that very thing.

Considering the breastplate of righteousness, I think of the clothing we must put on before the armor. As we walk in compassion, kindness, humility, gentleness, and patience, we position the breastplate of righteousness over our hearts so our very life is protected. These are God's virtues, and as we walk in them, we show that we belong to Jesus because we walk in His righteousness!

We again read about *peace.* Paul refers to this as the gospel of peace. Gospel means the teaching or revelation of Christ. I like that Paul illustrates this with our feet being fitted with peace. I take this literal as— everywhere we go, we are to reveal Christ through the peace He gives us. It is a true peace, and not the false peace that the world pushes.

The last piece of armor that I want to mention is the shield of faith. Did you catch what happens with faith? It bursts with hope. I picture faith as creating an invisible wall that encapsulates you so that no fiery arrows from the enemy can touch you. It is amazing. Let it be unto you according to your *faith* (Matthew 9:29).

Knowing these radical truths, we can win every battle we are faced with. As chosen and beloved daughters, let's be sure to clothe ourselves with heavenly garments and put on the armor of God daily.

Prayer:

Father, we thank you for this day. We rejoice in it because You made it. We clothe ourselves with Your garments of compassion, kindness, humility, gentleness, and patience. Bind these all in Your perfect love. We forgive those who have wronged us intentionally and unintentionally because You forgave us while we were still Your enemies. We choose to walk in Your truth, righteousness, and peace as we share Jesus everywhere we go! We love you and trust You. Amen.

*You did not choose me, but I chose you and appointed you so that
you might go and bear fruit–fruit that will last–and so that whatever
you ask in my name the Father will give you.*
John 15:16

Notes

_____

_____

_____

_____

_____

_____

_____

_____

Day 3

Before I formed you in the womb I knew you, before you were born
I set you apart; I appointed you as a prophet to the nations.

Jeremiah 1:5

 Eternity—the quality or state of being eternal; infinite time.[7]

I know that my heart yearns and hopes for eternity, but right now I cannot fathom it in its fullest sense. I believe most people want to be remembered forever, whether for good or for bad. I suppose this is because our Father set eternity in our hearts as He formed us. Perhaps you remember Ecclesiastes 3:11 says, "He has made everything beautiful in its time. He has also set eternity in the human heart; yet no one can fathom what God has done from beginning to end."

The seed of eternity has been planted in our hearts. If we seek to bring glory to any name other than Jesus, this eternal purpose will not be realized and we will be stuck feeling a sense of longing which cannot be satisfied. Have no fear, in the gospel of John, Jesus tells us how we can be brought to complete unity and fulfill our divine purpose.

John 17 is one of my very favorite chapters in the Bible. We get to know the precise words Jesus prayed for us! Can you believe it? I hope so. Jesus tells us what eternal life is in verse three, "Now this is eternal life: that they know you, the only true God, and Jesus Christ, whom you have sent."

Let's dig a little deeper and read John 17:13-25.

[7]www.meriam-webster.com

1. Why did Jesus say these specific things? (v 13)

2. Are we of this world? What do you think that means? (vv 14, 16)

3. Who sent us into the world? (v 18)

4. How are we sanctified? (v 19)

5. For whom did Jesus sanctify Himself?

6. Who is Jesus' prayer for? (v 20)

7. What is Jesus' prayer? (vv 21-24)

8. What equips us to be one with Jesus and God? (v 22)

9. What is the fruit of being brought to complete unity? (v 23b)

10. What do you think it means that the world does not know the Father?

11. What has Jesus made known to us and why? (v 26)

12. If we know the Father, what is in us? (v 26)

What an awesome prayer! It's a lot to ponder. If you need to wipe the sweat from your brow, go ahead and know you're not alone. Reading this prayer makes me feel like I have taken a ride on a rocket ship because it is so out of this world. Knowing how Jesus prayed for you and me over 2,000 years ago excites me to no end. Let's break it down.

Since John wrote the prayer of Jesus, I have to believe John overheard the words Jesus spoke to our Father. This prayer was not only for John, but it was for all of His disciples and for all of those who will confess Jesus as the Son of God and Savior of the world—hence, it includes you and me. Jesus wanted this tender and powerful prayer to be heard so that we could have the full measure of His joy within us.

We can have the full measure of Jesus' joy within us here on earth. We do not have to wait until we're in heaven. How do I know this? Jesus said, "I am coming to you [God] now, but I say these things while I am still in the world, **so that they**...". There ya go! He wanted us to know it is totally possible to have the FULL measure of His joy within us while we are still here on earth. Do you think you have ever tapped into even a half measure of His joy?

Jesus sends us into the world, not to be a part of the world and all of its lusts and passions, but to be set apart and sanctified. We are purified by the Word of God. It is absolute truth and it is trustworthy. All Scripture is God-breathed and is useful for teaching, rebuking, correcting and training in righteousness (2 Timothy 3:16). We should not make room for any other teachings or false truths. Jesus sanctified and purified Himself in the flesh so we would walk in the same unwavering manner.

Jesus didn't ask that we would be taken straight to heaven, but that we would be protected from the evil one as we are here on earth. Jesus knows the enemy wants to sift us like wheat and steal the abundant life that is ours if we are sanctified. Psalms 91 flashes through my mind as I think about the protection Jesus offers as we *say* "He is my refuge." There is action and faith required. We must speak out loud and testify that God is our safe haven in the storms of life and believe it. I see our Father appointing His ministering angels all around those who are not shaken by what is going on around them. We are protected from the pestilence and flaming arrows of the enemy. Remember that shield that pops up when we apply *faith* in the Holy One? We are in good hands.

I could write pages and pages about these few scriptures, but I will end with the glory and love of the Father. Jesus didn't ask our Holy Father to give us glory; Jesus said He **has given** us the glory that God gave Him (v 22). Wow. He already gave it to us so we would be one with Them. I'm no mathematician, but if I had to write this in algebraic form, this is how I'd write it:

Truth:

God = Love

God + Jesus = 1 = Jesus + Us

Then:

Jesus + Glory = God = Glory + Us

Bottom line, we fit in God's equation. We are One with Them, and Their glory enables us to be One. This is only possible because of God's love. Love holds it all together. God is love. Our goal is to be the love of God to the world. Jesus made our Father known in order that His love would be in us, which means, Jesus is in us. The book of First John talks more about what true love is. To dig deeper into what true love looks like, I recommend reading this entire epistle.

Ultimately, God's love placed eternity in our hearts. Everyone, regardless of receiving God or rejecting Him, has this place knit in the very depths of their being. I pray the love of the Father is received and poured out of you! It sets you apart in Him for all of eternity.

Those who trust in the Lord are like Mount Zion, which cannot be shaken
but endures forever. As the mountains surround Jerusalem, so the Lord
surrounds his people both now and forevermore.
Psalm 125:1-2

Notes

_____

_____

_____

_____

_____

_____

_____

_____

_____

_____

_____

_____

Day 4

If we confess our sins, he is faithful and just and will forgive
us our sins and purify us from all unrighteousness.
1 John 1:9

Forgiveness—the act of pardoning an offender.[8]

Forgiveness is powerful. By this act we are reconciled to our Holy Father. Forgiveness is a two-way street. It is something everyone has to receive and something everyone has to give. All have sinned and fall short of the glory of God (Romans 3:23).

Today, we are going to explore an incredible account in Luke. This story takes place in the home of Simon, the Pharisee, who had invited Jesus over for dinner. Jesus had already begun His ministry and many proclaimed Him to be a prophet, so I imagine Simon wanted to test this title. **Let's read Luke 7:36-50.**

1. **What motivated the sinful woman to come to the Pharisee's house? (v 37)**

2. **What did she bring with her? (v 37)**

3. **In your opinion, why do you think the woman wept?**

[8] www.jw.org

4. Challenge Question: Why do you think the sinful woman poured perfume on Jesus' feet?

5. What was the Pharisee's reaction to what he saw? (v 39)

6. How did Jesus respond to Simon's thoughts?

7. What were the customary things that Simon neglected to do to Jesus as He entered Simon's home? (vv 44-46)

8. What three things did the sinful woman do to Jesus' feet?

9. What was the reward for the love that she showed? (v 47)

10. What are the two things that Jesus said to the woman? (vv 48, 50)

♥ **What do you think your reaction would have been to hear the Messiah tell you, "Your sins are forgiven" and "Your faith has saved you; go in peace" in front of your accusers?**

At this point in Jesus' ministry, He had a following. The stories of His healings and miraculous dealings were spreading like wild fire throughout communities. People yearned to hear Him speak and be forever changed. Here in Luke, this particular sinful woman caught wind of where Jesus would be, and she couldn't resist showing up.

Many people suppose this woman was Mary, Lazarus' sister, who anointed Jesus' feet in the gospel of John. These are two different accounts and two different women. This story takes place earlier in Jesus' ministry, while the latter takes place at the end of His ministry just before His crucifixion.

The sinful woman—whose name we don't know—somehow learned Jesus would be in Simon's house. She *learned* and she *acted*. This is faith, y'all! She came in expectation as she brought her prized alabaster jar of perfume. This was an intentional act to bring something valuable to both men and women. It was as if she knew she would encounter her Redeemer and King that day. I believe her purposeful actions tenderized her heart for what was about to happen. Her act of faith had an eternal reward, and we get to learn from it too!

I am a visual learner, so as I read the story, I like to picture what is happening. I was imagining Jesus sitting in a chair at a table, but that didn't add up, so I asked the Holy Spirit to show me what this scene looked like. This is when the Holy Spirit helped me.

It was custom at that time to lay on pillows/cushions and lean on the left hand while eating with the right hand. This would have allowed Jesus' feet to be kicked out, and the woman to wet His feet from behind Him.

As you visualize the scene too, imagine how desperate for change this lady had to be. She didn't care who saw her or what they thought. She was *known* as a sinful woman, so entering the religious Pharisee's house was a bold step.

She purposefully put herself in a humble and lowly position as she wept at the beautiful feet of Him who was the Good News. She gave all of herself to Him as she dried His feet with her hair and then anointed His feet with her fragrant oil, a costly possession. I believe these acts were all received by Jesus as faith, hope, and love. She acted in faith as she went to meet Jesus in the Pharisee's house. She continued in faith as she courageously poured out the costly oil upon His feet, hoping He would receive this as a willing sacrifice, one not coerced. This was an act of love because it was a gift given with no expectation to be repaid. Jesus knows the intentions of our hearts, and we can be sure He knew her intention was pure.

I have to think she had faith in Jesus as the Christ, the Anointed One. With this being true, she must have hoped He could deliver her from any sin cycle. As she poured out her perfume, I'll bet she poured every drop, keeping nothing for herself.

All the meanwhile, Simon denied Jesus a holy kiss, anointing oil for his head, and water to wash His feet. These were all customary acts to show peace, respect, and love. Not only did Simon deny Jesus all of these easy things, but he denied Jesus as a prophet too.

Knowing Simon's judgmental thoughts, Jesus took the opportunity to respond. Jesus told a parable, and Simon was able to give a correct judgment regarding the scenario. Jesus affirmed him in this correct answer, however, He showed Simon how it applied to him and the woman. Simon did not judge himself, Jesus, or the woman rightly.

The Pharisee was blinded by self-righteousness, and he missed the opportunities of receiving needed forgiveness and administering love. His nearsightedness blinded him from rightly seeing the Sin Bearer and Son of God. The true Righteous One showed us that anyone who has faith in Him can receive the forgiveness that comes only from Him, thus producing acts of love which cover a multitude of sins!

I imagine hearing the words from the Sweetest Lips, "Your sins are forgiven" and "Your faith has saved you; go in peace" was more than she had hoped for. When we put our faith and trust in Jesus, that's exactly what we get— *more* than we can imagine! Put your faith and trust in Jesus today and expect to be forever changed!

This righteousness is given through faith in Jesus Christ to all who believe.
There is no difference between Jew and Gentile, for all have sinned and fall
short of the glory of God, and all are justified freely by his grace through
the redemption that came by Christ Jesus.
Romans 3:22-24

Notes

_____

_____

_____

_____

_____

Take my yoke upon you and learn from me, for I am gentle
and humble in heart, and you will find rest for your souls.
Matthew 11:29

 Gentle—having or showing a mild, kind,
or tender temperament or character.[9]

We can learn what gentle is by simply looking at Jesus. He is known as the Lamb of God for His gentle and docile character. He was gentle towards the woman caught in the act of adultery, the sinful woman anointing his feet, and the hemorrhaging woman who pushed through the crowd to touch His cloak. Jesus was gentle even to the point of death when they led Him to slaughter like a lamb (Isaiah 53:7). When we are gentle in heart, our actions and words follow suit and rest floods our souls.
Let's read Ephesians 4:1-16.

1. How does Paul refer to himself in verse one?

2. We are urged to live what type of life? (v 1)

3. How do we live a life worthy of the calling we have received? (vv 2,3)

4. How do we keep the unity of the Spirit? (v 3)

5. What were we called to? (vv 4-6)

6. To whom has Christ's grace been given? (v 7)

Does this remind you of Colossians 3:12? As I was reflecting on Ephesians, I had to do a double take because it sounded so familiar to Day 2. When we see repetition in the Bible—and we see that a lot—it means the subject matter is very important! God doesn't want us to miss what He is saying.

Paul starts this chapter referring to himself as a prisoner for the Lord, which implies his humble position compared to the King of kings. Paul knows he is owned by Christ, and he will not serve anyone but Him, and in doing so he urges us to live lives worthy of our calling.

Today we will focus on humility and gentleness. When we see gentleness in the Bible, much of the time it is paired with humility. The beauty of this is the portrait of Jesus I see. He is the epitome of these two virtues. Matthew 21:5 shows us how Jesus fulfilled what Zechariah (9:9) prophesied of Him:

9Say to Daughter Zion,
See, your king comes to you, gentle and riding on a donkey,
and on a colt, the foal of a donkey.

Jesus traded His King's robes for swaddling clothes when He first came to earth as a tiny babe. He was humble and gentle and showed us the way to our Father. Before He left this earth to sit at the right hand of our Father, He rode on a gentle donkey, once again taking a humble posture for all to witness.

Just recently, our children's ministry put on a skit called "A Young Girl's Donkey." A young girl had saved several denarii to purchase a horse *like the Roman soldiers rode.* However, she was disappointed to find out she could only afford a small donkey. She was so dismayed that she said to her mother sharply, "How can I become a respected rider? Famous people don't ride donkeys!"

At the end of the skit, the little girl returns to her mother shouting for joy, "The King has come. Hurry, let's go see Him!" To everyone's surprise, the child tells her mother as she sobs, "Look, Jesus is riding on my very own donkey."

Needless to say, hearts were gripped at how sweetly the children portrayed the reality of Jesus' humility and gentleness. And what better way to portray Jesus than through pure and meek children?

I find myself asking Jesus to give me His Spirit of gentleness in my actions, tone, and thoughts. At times when I need to redirect my daughters, I ask, "Have you just spoken in a gentle or harsh tone?" Proverbs gives us much wisdom, and 15:1 tells us that a gentle answer turns away wrath but a harsh word stirs up anger. I can recognize when anger is stirred up in my heart, and I am quickly reminded that a gentle response can effectively put out the fire of anger.

Jesus tells us to learn from Him, and He points out that His heart is gentle and humble. When we position our hearts to mirror His, our souls find rest. These attributes are essential in attaining unity in the body of Christ, which brings us to the full measure and maturity of Jesus. The full measure of Christ is what life is all about. This is His plan and purpose for everyone's life.

The fruits of the Spirit are love, joy, peace, forbearance, kindness, goodness, faithfulness, gentleness, and self-control. Against such things there is no law (Galatians 5:22-23). Each of these fruits were ripe in Jesus. I pray the same for you and me, but let's end today with a specific prayer for gentleness.

Prayer:

Holy Father, we thank You for Your words and Your life. We thank You for filling us with Your gentleness. As Elijah found You in the gentle whisper, let gentleness and humility be found in our hearts so that our thoughts, words, and actions turn away all wrath. Let Jesus' yoke be fastened upon us and His rest in our souls. We ask for unity among all of the body of Christ and for the body to be filled with the full measure of Your Son. We love You and we trust You. In Jesus' precious name we ask. Amen.

Let your gentleness be evident to all. The Lord is near.
Philippians 4:5

Notes

_____

_____

_____

_____

_____

_____

WEEK

Two

Day 1

Each of the four living creatures had six wings and was covered
with eyes all around, even under its wings. Day and night they never stop
saying: "HOLY, HOLY, HOLY, IS THE LORD GOD ALMIGHTY;
WHO WAS, AND IS, AND IS TO COME."
Revelation 4:8

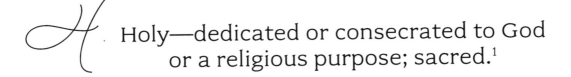

Holy—dedicated or consecrated to God or a religious purpose; sacred.[1]

The Apostle Peter spent his last years as a leader of the church in Rome. Many churches in Rome (now modern-day Turkey) were being persecuted, so he wrote a letter of instruction and encouragement urging them to remain steadfast to Jesus. **Let's read 1 Peter 1:1-25.**

1. According to verse thirteen, our minds should be in what state?

2. We should be what type of children? (v 14)

3. We conformed to evil desires when we lived in what condition? (v 14)

[1]www.lexico.org

4. How often are we to be holy? (v 15)

5. Why are we to be holy? (v 15)

6. What were we redeemed from? (v 18)

♥ What are some empty ways of life or empty traditions you inherited from your ancestors? Do you still hold on to those? Why or why not?

7. What were we redeemed with? (v 19)

8. For whose sake was Jesus revealed in these last times? (v 20)

9. How do we purify ourselves? (v 22)

10. What is the result of purifying ourselves? (v 22)

11. What endures forever? (vv 23, 25)

To me, the letters of Peter are a treasure. I relish his passion, loyalty, and love for Jesus. I perceive Peter as an over-the-top kind of guy who has a love for people. I can feel the joy of Jesus as I read his writings.

He addresses his readers as God's elect. He writes specifically to those who choose to believe and continue to live their lives *obediently* to Christ, sprinkled with His blood. It is because of God's great mercy and love that we were reborn into a living hope through Jesus' resurrection from the dead, so we receive an imperishable and incorruptible inheritance. What a hope we have in Jesus because of our Holy Father's faithfulness!

If we know and receive this hope, how could we not long to be obedient and holy as Jesus is? Peter instructs the elect/believers to have minds that are alert and fully sober. Another translation of this verse charges us to prepare our minds for action.

The definition for *alert* is quick to notice any unusual and potentially dangerous or difficult circumstances; vigilant.[2] A second definition is able to think clearly; intellectually active.[3] It makes sense for our minds to be vigilant and fully aware in order to be ready for action.

When Jesus met me in my bathroom in 2013, He opened my eyes to how I was living for the world instead of obediently to Him. During this time, I struggled over the question if I should drink alcohol or not. I especially enjoyed drinking wine. Prior

[2] www.yahoo.com [3] www.lexico.com

to having an intimate relationship with Jesus, I did not have self-control to stop drinking once I started. Celebrations and holidays didn't seem complete without an alcoholic beverage in hand. I reasoned, if other Christians could drink, then so could I. I compared my life to others' lives instead of God's Word. However, the scripture about being fully sober tugged at my heart, because I knew if I drank—even one glass of wine—my mind would not be alert.

"How can I pray if I am not sober?" I asked myself. How can the Holy Spirit dwell within me if I am drunk or *buzzing*? These questions were impressed upon my heart. Every time I read this verse, I have peace in my decision not to drink alcohol.

I finally understood what this scripture meant for *my* life. I had to listen to what Jesus was saying to me and not compare my walk with Him to anyone else's. My struggles and weaknesses are different. Most of all, I want to be obedient and holy in His sight.

Someone once asked me, "Where does it stop? Can I not have chocolate or caffeine?" Answering some questions may help: Is your mind fully alert and sober on caffeine or chocolate? Do you lack self-control when it comes to their consumption? Can you pray with a clear mind? Have you asked the Holy Spirit to reveal if there is an idolization of these things?

I no longer live in ignorance or chained to evil desires I once had when I lived blinded to His truth. God is *holy*, which means He is not like anyone else. He is set apart and other than. I want to be holy because He is holy. Leviticus 11:44 says, "I am the Lord your God; consecrate yourselves and be holy, because I am holy." It is enough for me to be holy just because He is holy, and He said so.

I often hear Christians give holiness a bad reputation. They portray being holy as a negative trait. I have even heard renowned men of God say, "Don't be so holy." It is important to see the enemy's schemes here. God said we are to be holy because He is holy. This is a good label, but if Satan can put doubt in our minds or taint the term *holy*, it can influence disobedience and hinder our relationship with our loving Father, which is exactly what the enemy wants.

One way I like to test holiness in my life is by self-reflecting and asking, "Am I being obedient to God's Word?" If so, I continue in what I am doing regardless of the back-lash from people. If I have imposed rules upon myself— I cannot sleep in, or I cannot go to a certain place— I may have slipped into legalism, an excessive adherence to law or formula. I believe people intertwine holiness and legalism. This mistake can lead to sin and disobedience. We may begin to feel superior to others and push them away from a meaningful relationship with Jesus.

♥ **Do you view holiness as a positive character trait or do you separate yourself from holiness?**

At times, people feel judgment when they compare their lives of sin to a holy life and they feel guilt and shame. Instead of conforming and yielding to a life like Christ's, they denigrate others as self-righteous and reject holiness for themselves.

All in all, holiness is a wonderful thing. God is holy. Because of His holiness we have eternal life.

Prayer Moment: If someone comes to mind who lives a life in fear or rebellion to holiness, pray and ask for the Holy Spirit to reveal the love and sacrifice of Jesus which will lead to repentance, salvation, and holiness.

I like to imagine the vision Isaiah had of the Lord sitting on His throne, high and lifted up while His robe filled the temple. And Isaiah heard the seraphim calling out to one another, "Holy, holy, holy is the Lord of hosts, The whole earth is full of His glory." Isaiah recognized his state of unholiness and cried out specifically about his unclean lips. In response, the seraphim flew to him with a fiery coal taken from God's altar and touched his mouth with it, saying, "See, this has touched your lips; your guilt is taken away and your sin atoned for" (Isaiah 6).

Isaiah's vision and encounter gave him hope and pointed forward to the salvation through Jesus' everlasting atonement, available for the whole world. John the Baptist prophesied to this as well when he said, "I baptize you with water. But one who is more powerful than I will come, the straps of whose sandals I am not worthy to untie. He will baptize you with the Holy Spirit and fire" (Luke 3:16).

Jesus came from God's altar and cleanses not only our lips, but also our souls! He revealed Himself in these last times for *our* sakes. He poured out His blood and life for us, so we would be redeemed and rescued from perishing. We know that material things spoil and fade away, but the salvation and inheritance we find in Christ never loses its power or victory. We are made holy through His precious, eternal blood, much better than silver and gold.

Jesus is the Word. As we read the Word, the Holy Bible, we are literally reading and absorbing Jesus into our body, soul, and mind. As we choose to obey the truth, we become pure. This purity produces a sincere love for one another, and we are able to love one another deeply from an intimate place in our hearts where Jesus Himself resides.

Jesus said He is the way, the truth, and the life. It is through Him, the living enduring Word, that we learn who God is and are reconciled to Him (John 1:1, John 14:6, 1 Peter 1:25). As we end here today, ask the Holy Spirit to reveal any empty ways of life you may be holding on to and cast them upon Jesus as He unchains you from the former ways of life when you lived in ignorance! He is faithful and will give you His very own holiness.

Sing to him, sing praises to him; tell of all his wonderful acts.
Glory in his holy name; let the hearts of those who seek the LORD rejoice.
1 Chronicles 16:9-10

Notes

_____

_____

_____

_____

_____

_____

_____

_____

_____

_____

_____

_____

Who shall separate us from the love of Christ?
Shall trouble or hardship or persecution or famine
or nakedness or danger or sword?
Romans 8:35

 Inseparable—unable to be separated
or treated separately.[4]

When I hear the word *inseparable*, a friend pops in mind whom I've known since I was three years old. We went through pre-school, elementary, middle, and high-school together. Not only my parents, but also our peers referred to us as *inseparable* because we were generally always found at the same place at the same time. Now we are grown and have separate lives, but inseparable was true of us when we were young.

In today's terms of being inseparable, my wedding comes to mind. The pastor referenced Mark 10:9 which says, "Therefore what God has joined together, let no one separate." Today, we are going to explore the inseparable love of Christ. **Let's read Romans 8.**

1. Is there condemnation for those who are in Christ Jesus? (v 1)

2. What does the law of the Spirit do through Christ Jesus? (v 2)

[4] Ibid

3. Jesus condemned sin in the flesh in order that what may happen? (v 4)

4. What does the mind governed by the Spirit produce? (v 6b)

5. If Christ is in you, the Spirit gives what? Why? (v 10b)

6. Those who are led by the Spirit of God are called what? (v 14)

7. If we share in Christ's sufferings, what else will we share? (v 17)

8. Our present sufferings are not worth comparing with what? (v 18)

9. What will the creation be brought into? (v 21)

10. What does God do for those who love Him? (v 28)

11. What did God do for those He foreknew? (vv 29, 30)

12. Verse 33 asks a question. What is the answer?

13. Who then is the one who condemns? (v 34)

14. Who is interceding for us? (v 34)

Wow. Are you encouraged yet? Paul asks a lot of rhetorical questions in this letter. I believe he asked these questions to direct our attention to the eternal life, peace, justification, righteousness, glory, and overwhelming victory we have through Jesus Christ.

Jesus' death and resurrection fully met the righteous requirement for us who live according to His Spirit. Hallelujah! The price we owed was wholly, entirely, absolutely, and totally met and paid by our King, Jesus. Since He condemned sin and death in His flesh, we can have life and peace.

There is no longer condemnation for those who are in Jesus. The guilty verdict that was ours has now been placed on sin and death. Those in Christ have been pardoned. With this acquittal, we have an obligation, a commitment, and a duty to live by the Spirit. This means to live in love, joy, peace, patience, goodness, gentleness, kindness, faithfulness, and self-control. We are children of God—His heirs and co-heirs with Jesus.

Although we receive these great titles, we are still prone to afflictions of many kinds, but we can take hope and confidence in the glory that will be revealed in us. We are not alone in the trials and anguish. Jesus overcame the wilderness and all of Satan's propositions, He overcame the hypocrisy and judgment of the Pharisees, and He overcame death and sin as He poured out His life for all. He lived, died, and most importantly, rose again three days later. This resurrection life and glory is ours as His co-heir. Creation itself also waits in eager expectation to be unfettered and brought into the freedom and glory of the children of God.

As we hope and wait for what is to come, we can be encouraged furthermore by the Spirit. When we seem to have reached the end of our rope and do not know how or what to pray, the Spirit Himself intercedes for us through wordless groans in accordance with the will of God. And still yet, we know completely that God works IN ALL things for the good of those who love Him. It is comforting to know that God is IN it with us. He knows every detail of the past, present, and future.

"For I know the plans I have for you," declares the Lord, "plans to prosper you and not to harm you, plans to give you hope and a future (Jeremiah 29:11). God's plans concerning our future have not changed!

I heard a woman of God say that Jesus revealed to her, "He is the storm." What an amazing perspective! What comes to mind is the scene of Jesus sleeping in the stern of the boat and His disciples frantic as the storm raged. It is perplexing to think Jesus Himself was the storm. He knew exactly what was happening, and He did care. He wasn't going to let His sheep be swept or carried away by the waves or the wind. Not then, and not now. "He is the LORD our God; his judgments are in all the earth. He remembers his covenant forever, the promise he made, for a thousand generations," (Psalm 105:7-8).

We have been foreknown, called, justified, and glorified. So regardless of accusations brought against us, we know God has already justified us. We have been vindicated and made blameless because of the righteousness of Jesus—His precious Son. Not only does the Spirit plead for us, but Jesus also intercedes for us at God's right hand! So knowing all of this, let me ask: Who shall separate us from the love of Christ? If no one can condemn us or bring a charge against us, no one can separate us from His love. God did not give up His Son for a hollow inheritance. He gave up His Son so we could become His inheritances and His heirs. No president or king, pandemic, Marxist group, or financial hardship can separate us from the love of Christ. If Christ is in you, the Spirit gives LIFE because of righteousness!

Rebuke the lies of the enemy who says otherwise. Satan's words do not create life, righteousness, or peace. They bring despair, confusion, and death. Whatever circumstances are present in your life, you can rest assured that the love of our Father is inseparable. The love of Jesus is inseparable. If feelings of anxiousness or hopelessness try to invade your soul, declare the words of truth and grace found in Romans. They are your words to live by, for, and through.

For the Lord watches over the way of the righteous,
but the way of the wicked leads to destruction.
Psalm 1:6

Notes

_____

_____

Day 3

I have told you this so that my joy may be in you
and that your joy may be made complete.
John 15:11

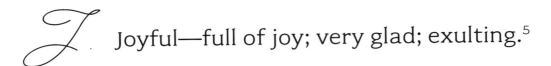 Joyful—full of joy; very glad; exulting.[5]

There is nothing like the joy of the Lord. It can carry you through the good times and the bad. **Let's read John 15:1-17 and see how we receive Jesus' complete joy.**

1. According to verse one, how are Jesus and His Father described?

2. What does the Father do? (v 2)

3. What are we instructed to do in verse four?

4. To what are we likened in verse five?

5. What happens to the branches that do not remain in Jesus? (v 6)

[5] www.webstersdictionary1828.com

6. What is the result of remaining in Jesus and who receives the glory? (vv 7, 8)

7. How do we remain in Jesus' love? (v 10)

8. How is our joy made complete? (vv 10, 11)

I am so thankful we have Jesus' words and teachings to reflect on and live by. Even though He spoke these words thousands of years ago, they are just as relevant and true today. I find it interesting that keeping Jesus' commands is the key to having Jesus' complete joy. When we keep His commands, we remain in His love and then have His complete joy.

A dear friend recently recommended a book, *Heaven: an Unexpected Journey*[6], by Jim Woodford with Dr. Thom Gardner. Jim details his unexpected eleven-hour experience in Heaven, and I had to share this definition of joy. Jim writes, "The tall warrior angel described joy as living on the edge of a huge laugh motivated by a constant awareness of the presence of God." I cannot think of a more heavenly definition of joy. If you have not read this book, it is a must. I thank our Heavenly Father for giving Jim this unforgettable experience. He knew this would bring a renewed sense of joy, faith, and hope to those who heard this testimony! God's lovingkindness never ends.

[6]Woodford, Jim, and Gardner, Dr. Thom. Destiny Image, Inc. 2017. 82.

Continuing with the subject of joy, Psalm 34 is a wonderful parallel verse which echoes Jesus' teaching in John. The entire Psalm affirms Jesus' teaching, but I am going to highlight a few verses here:

⁴ I sought the LORD, and he answered me;
He delivered me from all my fears.
⁵ Those who look to him are radiant; their faces are never covered with shame.
⁶ This poor man called, and the LORD heard him;
He saved him out of all his troubles.
⁷ The angel of the LORD encamps around those who fear him,
And he delivers them.
⁸ Taste and see that the LORD is good; blessed is the one who takes refuge in him.
⁹ Fear the LORD, you his holy people, for those who fear him lack nothing.

Wow. Have you ever likened the fear of the Lord to having His complete joy? Those who fear Him lack nothing! Those who fear Him and keep His commands remain in His love and have His complete joy. Those who look to Him are *radiant*, and their faces are never covered with shame. This is why the first commandment is so important. Love the Lord your God with all your heart and with all your soul and with all your mind (Matthew 22:37). God's word gives us full instructions on how to please Him and how to receive complete joy in Him.

♥ **Remember a time you walked in the fear of the Lord and received His complete joy as a result. List it below.**

There was a time early in my marriage when I had not been completely honest with my husband. I had kept a matter of my past hidden from him. This deception, which I had justified as "nobigdeal", weighed heavier on my shoulders the deeper my relationship with Christ became. My mind reeled with possible scenarios if I confessed.

When God's Word became real in my heart, I knew I had to tell the whole truth. I feared being rejected and losing our marriage, but most of all, I feared losing my relationship with my Heavenly Father. I sought the Lord, and He gave me courage to be completely honest with my husband. God delivered me from all of my fears and gave me His radiance and joy. I no longer felt the heaviness of guilt and shame. My husband forgave me for not being honest, and our relationship became stronger than ever as we sought the Lord together.

My friend, I hope you experience the pruning love of the Father that brings His extensive joy. There is nothing worth more than the Father's love. Follow His commands and be ready to live on the edge of a huge laugh motivated by a constant awareness of the presence of God.

Give me understanding, so that I may keep your law and obey it with all my heart.
Psalm 119:34

Notes

_____

_____

_____

_____

Those who are kind benefit themselves,

but the cruel bring ruin on themselves.

Proverbs 11:17

 Kind—having or showing a friendly, generous, sympathetic, or warm-hearted nature.[6]

It is God's lovingkindness that draws us to Him, and it is His divine power that has given us everything we need to be effective in life through the knowledge of Him. **Let's read 2 Peter 1:1-11.**

1. What is granted to us in the knowledge of God and Jesus our Lord? (vv 2, 3)

2. What are we to add to our faith? (vv 5-7)

3. If we lack these qualities, what does it render us? (v 9)

4. What are the promises for those who practice these qualities? (vv 10, 11)

[6]www.thefreedictionary.com

Simon Peter, a bondservant of Christ, shows us that kindness is one of the virtues that we must add to our faith. Without it, we are ineffective and unproductive in our knowledge of our Savior. The true revelation and knowledge of Him is what gives us everything we need to succeed in this turbulent life.

It takes my breath away to realize we can participate in His divine nature as we bring His kingdom on earth as it is in heaven. Kindness or love is one of the ways we display heaven.

Peter tells us that as long as we practice goodness, knowledge, self-control, perseverance, godliness, mutual affection (brotherly kindness), and love, we will *never* stumble. This sounds like a recipe for perfection, and the measurements are ever-increasing. If you have a hard time with rendering kindness, start off with a dash here and there. After you are comfortable with a dash, graduate to a teaspoon. Then a tablespoon. The tablespoon will then become a heaping tablespoon, a cup, a gallon, and then a liter, until you are flowing endlessly in the kindness of God. If we find ourselves stumbling, we can look at these qualities and measure what we are lacking or not increasing in.

♥ **Are you satisfied with where you are in your knowledge of God and our Lord Jesus? If not, ask the Lord what virtue needs growth.**

Job soberingly states that, "Anyone who withholds kindness from a friend forsakes the fear of the Almighty" (Job 6:14). Without kindness, we lack true wisdom which is the fear of the Lord. Without wisdom, we lack the knowledge of who God and Jesus are and it renders us ineffective in our divine nature and calling. Kindness is one of the keys to the kingdom of God.

♥ **Are you satisfied with the measure of kindness in your life? What are some ways you can grow in kindness?**

Kindness is not something that we should seldom display. Some groups practice random acts of kindness, but I believe kindness should be more consistent. I want it to pour out of me in every instance and not haphazardly. The Lord will use every measure of kindness we give to others to draw them into His kingdom.

Prayer:

Father, I thank You for Your lovingkindness that drew my heart to Yours. While I was still in my transgressions, You sent Your Son to rescue me. Add Your kindness to my faith. Let it overflow onto all I meet and in every circumstance. I want to walk in the wisdom and knowledge of You as I revere You as Lord of my life. Amen.

But when the kindness and love of God our Savior appeared, he saved us,
not because of righteous things we had done, but because of his mercy.
Titus 3:4-5a

Notes

_____

_____

_____

_____

As the Father has loved me, so have I loved you.

Now remain in my love.

John 15:9

Love—a strong feeling of affection and concern toward another person, as that arising from kinship or close friendship.[7]

This is what Christianity is all about. The more I come to know the Lord, I see His rich love in everything He does. You know the song, "Jesus Loves Me?" I love the verse, Jesus loves me, *this I know.* Once we come to know His love, the rest is His story!

His love changes everything. So the question is, do you know His love for *you*? Grabbing hold of this truth is life-altering. His love unlocks heaven inside of those who believe and receive it. **Let's read John 3:14-21.**

1. Why was the Son of Man lifted up? (v 15)

2. Why did God give His one and only Son? (v 16)

3. How do unbelievers stand? (v 18)

[7]Ibid

4. Who hates the light? Why? (v 20)

For God so *loved* the *world* that He **gave** His one and only Son. Jesus is and was the best gift to ever be given, and He was given in love. He was **sent** to save the world, not punish it. Those who believe in God's love through His Son Jesus, will inherit eternal life! Jesus took the condemnation for those who believe in Him. Whoever does not believe will be condemned.

We get a snapshot of what love looks like all throughout the Bible, but the Gospel of John, 1 John, and 1 Corinthians have specific parameters to help us to know if we are walking in love. For the most part, 1 John recaps what was stated in the Gospel of John. The author doesn't identify himself, but it is thought to be the Apostle John. He similarly shares that whoever does not love does not know God, because God is love (1 John 4:8).

> *10This is love: not that we loved God, but that he loved us and*
> *sent his Son as an atoning sacrifice for our sins. 11Dear friends,*
> *since God so loved us, we also ought to love one another.*
> *12No one has ever seen God; but if we love one another, God lives*
> *in us and his love is made complete in us. 1 John 4:10-12*

In order for God's love to be made complete in us, we have to believe that He loved us first. Once we have recognized and received His love, we can render His love to others.

5. Do you believe that Jesus loves *you*?

6. Do you find it easier to believe that Jesus loves others vs yourself? If so, why?

7. Do you love others? What does your love look like?

When it comes to loving others, the Holy Spirit has helped me to recognize if the intentions of my heart are of love or not. He asks me simple questions. Was this love or selfishness? Was this love or control? Was this love or jealousness? I can measure the intentions of my heart by 1 Corinthians 13:4-8. If love wasn't the motivating factor, I can repent and do it again. I am not afraid to bring my deeds into the light and be made complete by Him. What I do is plainly seen by Him, and I want others to see *Him* clearly through my actions.

I have also come to learn when I am not acting in love, it is because my idea of His love for me is skewed to some degree. The root always comes from a place where I haven't received His love for me. When I let Him take me back to that broken place (this may be needed more than once), I can recognize and receive His love, so I am able to render His love to others effectively. God makes it simple for us—only believe. Believe it in all of its depth, width, and height for YOU.

And I pray that you, being rooted and established in love, may have power,
together with all the Lord's holy people, to grasp how wide and long and high and deep
is the love of Christ, and to know this love that surpasses knowledge—that you
may be filled to the measure of all the fullness of God.
Ephesians 3:17b-19

Notes

_____

_____

_____

_____

_____

_____

_____

_____

_____

_____

_____

_____

_____

WEEK

Three

For you created my inmost being; you knit me together in my

mother's womb. I praise you because I am fearfully and wonderfully

made; your works are wonderful, I know that full well.

Psalms 139:13-14

Masterpiece—an outstanding work of art or craft. The greatest work, as of an artist. Something superlative or unmatched of its kind.[1]

God is the Master Craftsman, and He master-crafted YOU in the image of Himself. You are His masterpiece. **Let's read Psalm 139:1-18.**

1. What has the Lord done to get to know you? (v 1)

♥ Do you search and seek God to get to know Him? If so, how?

2. When does the Lord know what we are going to say? (v 4)

[1]www.thefreedictionary.com

3. What does verse five mean to you?

4. Where is God's Spirit and presence? (vv 8-12)

5. Who created you? (v 13)

6. What two adjectives describe God's craftmanship of you? (v 14) What does this mean to you?

7. How many thoughts does the Lord have concerning you? (vv 17, 18)

♥ Do you know full well that you are wonderfully and fearfully made? What does this mean to you personally?

Psalm 139 is spectacular. This psalm gives such intimate detail on who God is and how He works. He is active and engaged in our lives. He searches us and knows us better than we know ourselves. He literally can finish our sentences, because He knows what we're going to say before it's on our tongues. He knows our hearts.

God is not far away or distant, as the enemy wants us to believe. David records that God is everywhere. He is omnipresent, which means He is present everywhere simultaneously. He never leaves us.

I love verse five of this Psalm. I interpret this as God has protected me from my past and I do not have to worry about the future because He is already there. His hand is upon me, instilling His power and anointing to walk in His ways. This coincides with Romans 8:28, which promises in all things God works for the good of those who love Him. Again, we see God is engaged and active in our life and in each of its details.

There are many ways the enemy can discourage us, but one way he lies to some is by saying, "Your life was an accident." If you were *unplanned* by your parents, the enemy especially loves to hurl this assault at you. The devil tries to imply that your biological parents were the only ones responsible—or irresponsible—for your creation. However, God's Word says that *He* created your inmost being and *He* knit you together in your mother's womb. The Creator of heaven and earth and all that is in them, intentionally and purposefully master-crafted YOU!

When His Word says He *fearfully* made you, it means you are not lacking anything! It doesn't matter if someone wants to label you as handicapped or having special needs, YOU ARE LACKING NO GOOD THING. You are FULL of wonder and awe because the Master Potter made you exquisitely for display of His character and glory! There will be hardship in our lives, but in all these things we are more than conquerors through Him who loved us (Romans 8:37).

Lastly, when the enemy tries to convince you that nobody cares for you, read verses seventeen and eighteen. God cannot get you off of His mind. As I look out of my window, I can see sand all around. The task of numbering the grains of sand would be impossible—far too much to record. I would quickly lose count. God says He has more thoughts towards you than this! He is a caring God who wants you to have the abundant and eternal life that His Son, Jesus, won for you. He is with you and He is for you.

Prayer:

Almighty God, You are the Master Craftsman. I thank You for carefully and intentionally creating me as You continue to lay Your mighty hand upon me. Your concern and care are towards me, and I am ever grateful for this fact. Show me how to seek You and know You, as You search me and know me. Teach me how to value and use the qualities and gifts You have intricately woven in me. Thank You for creating me. I love You. In Jesus' name, amen.

> *You, Lord, keep my lamp burning;*
> *my God turns my darkness into light.*
> *Psalm 18:28*

Notes

_____

_____

_____

_____

_____

_____

_____

_____

_____

_____

Day 2

I will lead the blind by ways they have not known, along unfamiliar paths
I will guide them; I will turn the darkness into light before them and make the
rough places smooth. These are the things I will do; I will not forsake them.

Isaiah 42:16

N Not forsaken—not abandoned, casted away, or left behind. A few synonyms for forsaken are: deserted, forgotten, rejected, neglected, unattended, and discarded.[2]

God promises to *never* forsake you. God must have designed *Not Forsaken* to follow *Masterpiece* because these are so parallel in their messages. We will continue to look at how wonderful God the Creator is, and what amazing things He will do for those who follow Him. **Let's read one of my favorites, Isaiah 42:1-17.**

1. What will God's Servant bring to the nations? (v 1)

2. How will He bring forth justice? (v 3b)

3. What are the things that God does, according to verse five?

[2]www.meriam-webster.com

4. In what does the Lord call you? (v 6a)

5. List at least three things the Lord will do according to verses six and seven.

6. What does God do before new things spring into being? (v 9)

7. What instruction does verse ten give?

8. What happens after praises and glory are given to God? (v 13)

9. What does God do for those in verse sixteen? What does this mean to you personally?

10. What happens to those who trust in anything other than God? (v 17)

Again, Isaiah gives us an accurate message from God. Even as He promised in His Word, God told Isaiah what would happen before it came about. Isaiah relayed a perfect description of what Jesus would do before He walked on the earth. Isn't it encouraging to know that God speaks beforehand and tells us of things to come?

When we believe in Jesus, His attributes and privileges become our very own! Just as God's Holy Spirit was upon Jesus, His Holy Spirit is upon those who are born again, and He leads those who do not know Him into His truth. As we follow Jesus, who brings forth justice faithfully, we too bring forth justice. You can trust that we have also been called into His righteousness.

God takes us by the hand and keeps us. This is such an amazing promise. We do not have to live in fear that God will lose us. As a child, I remember having the fear of being lost or kidnapped. If we were at an amusement park or even a grocery store, I would consciously make note of where security guards were if I should lose my mom.

Also, when walking home from school alone, I would constantly check my surroundings and pay special attention to white vans. I had heard horrible stories of kidnappers throwing small children in white vans, and I was terrified this would be my fate.

As a follower and believer of Jesus Christ, we do not have to live in fear, especially of being lost. Our attentive Father in heaven will not allow anyone to snatch us out of His hand (John 10:28-30).

God watches over our very lives as He lights up our inner being. Matthew 6:22 actually says that the eye is the lamp of the body. I marvel at this illustration and reality. God says He opens blind eyes. He does this both physically and spiritually. God is a miracle worker, and He still gives sight to those who were once blind. He also gives us spiritual eyes to clearly see and understand His Word, the source of eternal life and light.

As we read God's Word, it is important to make note when He gives us instructions. In Isaiah 42, verses ten through twelve, we are told to sing a new song and give praise to the Lord, to raise voices and shout from the mountaintops. Rejoice and give glory to the Lord!

Do you consider yourself a soft-spoken or quiet person? The Lord tells us to break those barriers and let our voices loose for His glory. When we do so, the Lord marches out as our champion! Our praises stir up His zeal like a warrior. He responds to our praise and rejoicing over Him with shouting and victory over His enemies! He moves mountains that may be hindering our journey with Him, He turns the darkness into light, and He makes the rough places smooth.

These promises were a lifeline to me at one point in my life. I remember crying these very words in my prayers to Him. I reminded Him and myself of His promises, and I saw them all come to pass. Painful memories were replaced with joyful ones previously hidden, and new healthy thought patterns replaced the toxic ones. He still continues to smooth out the rough places in my life and in the lives of loved ones. He is so gracious and merciful.

Even with this amazing news, there are still those who put their trust and hope in things other than Jesus. This is a grave mistake that leads to death and shame. But those who trust in Jesus will never be put to shame (Isaiah 45:17; 1 Peter 2:6). We will not be forsaken!

My Father, who has given them to me, is greater than all; no one can snatch them out of my Father's hand. I and the Father are one.

John 10:29-30

Notes

_____

_____

_____

_____

_____

_____

_____

_____

_____

_____

_____

_____

_____

Don't you know that you yourselves are God's temple
and that God's Spirit dwells in your midst?
1 Corinthians 3:16

 Ordained—to invest officially (as by the laying on of hands) with ministerial or priestly authority.[3]

We read on day one of this week that God lays His hand on us (Psalm 139:5). When we surrender our life to Jesus as our Lord and Savior, we become the temple of God. His Spirit lives in us and His hand is upon us! **Read 1 Peter 2:4-10.**

1. Who is the living Stone? (v 4)

2. What are we like? (v 5)

3. What do the living stones build and what is their purpose? (v 5)

[3]Ibid

4. Will those who trust in Jesus ever be put to shame? (v 6)

5. How do those who believe consider this Stone? (v 7a)

6. What does the Stone become to those who do not believe? (vv 7b, 8)

7. What does it mean to stumble? (v 8b)

♥ How do you consider the Stone?

Just as God considers His Son, Jesus, as a precious living Stone, we too are considered chosen, royal, holy, and special as well. He has laid His righteous right hand upon those who trust in this precious Cornerstone. He has ordained as a holy priesthood those who are being built into a glorious house for His Spirit. Every believer contains a portion of Jesus inside of them, and as we come together, we shine brighter as we declare His praises!

To be a royal priesthood and set apart as holy, means to revere the name of God and walk in the fear of the Lord. We choose to follow His commands and live in a way that is counter to the culture of this world and its dark ways. We love the Lord our God with all of our hearts and love others above ourselves. We seek truth, justice, and righteousness. We simply live like Jesus.

Those who do not believe stumble because they do not obey His words and commands. To unbelievers, His ways are often viewed as out of date, old fashioned, and unimportant. This stumbling could be prevented if they would choose to soften their hearts. The Lord makes His Word understandable to the simple. You do not need a pastor or theologian to understand the message of God's grace and mercy. His Holy Spirit will give you understanding if you seek Him with all of your heart.

I can remember when the Living Stone was once a stumbling block for me. My heart was once hardened to His ways. I actually said I believed, but my actions proved otherwise. After returning to God and seeking Him through reading the Bible, I heard Him speak to me very clearly in my bathroom. He said, "You say you believe, but when it comes down to it, you take the road widely traveled versus the narrow road." I wept because it was the truth. I couldn't argue. I decided then and there to follow Him no matter the cost. It has been a life-giving decision. By His mercy and calling, I now walk in His wonderful light!

♥ Do you remember the day you accepted His call to walk in His light? If so, share about that day. If not, would you like to walk in His light today? Talk to your Bible study leader now or, if you are completing this study solo, send me an email: Heather@JesusIsHealer.com

He himself bore our sins in his body on the cross, so that we might die to sins and live for

righteousness; by his wounds you have been healed. For you were like sheep going astray,

but now you have returned to the Shepherd and Overseer of your souls.

1 Peter 2:24-25

Notes

_____

_____

_____

_____

_____

_____

_____

_____

_____

_____

_____

_____

_____

Since you are precious and honored in My sight, and because I love you,
I will give people in exchange for you, nations in exchange for your life.

Isaiah 43:4

Precious—of high cost or worth; valuable: precious jewels.[4]

By now, have you noticed that the Word of God is reciprocal? Jesus is the precious Living Stone, and He was given in exchange for our souls. Likewise, we (believers) are like living stones being built up into a spiritual house, and we give our lives to Him. God delights Himself in us and sings over us, and we delight ourselves in Him and sing a new song unto Him. God gives us the crown of life, and we lay that crown down at His feet. What a beautiful exchange—one called love. **Let's continue to read His love letter to us in Isaiah 43:1-7.**

1. What instruction are you given in verse one? Why?

♥ What does it mean to you that the Creator of heaven and earth calls you by name?

2. When will God be with you? (v 2)

3. What will be the outcome when you walk through fire? (v 2)

4. What is given for your ransom and in your stead? (v 3)

5. Why does God give people and nations in exchange for your life? (v 4)

6. What are you instructed in verse five?

7. You were created for what purpose? (v 7b)

Isaiah starts Chapter 43 in a very assuring statement, "But now, this is what the Lord says—." If the Lord said it, we can believe it. He is a Man of His word! We do not have to fear because God has redeemed us; He has purchased us with the blood of His Son! We can rest assured that we are His and, as we walk through the storms of life and the fiery trials, we will not be overtaken by the raging waters or the heat that comes upon us. He calls our name and lifts our heads and holds our hand as we walk *through* it all *together.*

One of my favorite childhood books is, *"We're Going on a Bear Hunt."* I love the imagery the story lends to God's Word. As the family is going on a bear hunt, they repeatedly state, "We're not scared." Then, at one point, they come to a river and exclaim, "Uh-uh! A river! A deep cold river. We can't go over it. We can't go under it. Oh no! We've got to go through it." As this determined family comes to each trial, they realize they can't go over it, they can't go under it, they have to go *through* it! The Good News that Isaiah proclaims is that we have One greater than us who goes *through it with us* so we do not give up. We overcome hand in hand with the One who overcame.

Because God deems you as precious and because He loves you, He gives people and nations in exchange for your life. God is the most adoring and attentive Father to His children. Those who reject God and His ways are not His children, and do not receive the promises of God. The evil are given up for the righteous. Proverbs 11:8 says, "The righteous is delivered out of trouble, and the wicked cometh in his stead." Proverbs 21:8 continues, "The wicked become a ransom for the righteous, and the faithless for the upright."

We can see this promise played out in Exodus. Egypt was full of witchcraft, paganism, and idolatry. They worshipped nearly everything under the sun, including the sun itself. God fulfilled His promise and delivered Israel out of the bonds of Egypt through His faithful servant Moses. Pharaoh had opportunities to accept God as the One true God, but his rejection of God and his wickedness brought trouble to the point of death upon him and his followers (Exodus 14).

It is also important to know the meaning of the names Jacob and Israel. Jacob is the son of Isaac, the son of Abraham. Jacob, Abraham's grandson, wrestled with God (Genesis 32). In this wrestling and striving, Jacob did not give up. Although his hip was dislocated and thrust out of its socket, Jacob did not give up. He continued until he received a blessing from the Lord. It is at that point that Jacob's name was changed to Israel which in Hebrew means to *wrestle.*

God made a covenant with Abraham, Isaac, and Jacob/Israel. As believers in Jesus Christ, we inherit the promises of Israel. Continuing in this same excitement is God's promise in Joshua 21:45 which states, "Not one of all the Lord's good promises to Israel failed; every one was fulfilled." I hope that you, as a child of God, realize that you walk in the fulfilled promises of Israel! We will come to struggles and wrestling matches in life here on earth, but we do not give up. We go through it and come out as champion victors so we can give all honor and glory to God!

You are worthy, our Lord and God, to receive glory and honor and power, for you created all things, and by your will they were created and have their being.
Revelation 4:11

Notes

_____

_____

_____

_____

_____

_____

_____

_____

_____

The Lord is my shepherd, I lack nothing. He makes me lie down in green
pastures, he leads me beside quiet waters, he refreshes my soul.
Psalm 23:1-3a

 Quiet—free of turmoil and
agitation; calm.[5]

This is an amazing promise and psalm that ushers in the quiet assurance and calm of
God. This is a great psalm to memorize and know in the depths of your soul. It is full
of praise for Yahweh, the One true God. **Let's read Psalm 23.**

1. How is the Lord described in verse one?

2. What promise(s) do you read in verse one? Do you believe this?

**3. Challenge Question: What significance or symbolism do you find with a sheep
lying down in green pastures? How does this relate to your life?**

♥ What promise(s) mean the most to you of verses 1-3?

♥ What do you think the Lord has set on the table He has prepared for you? What spiritual enemies do you think are present as a witness to His goodness?

4. How often does His goodness and love follow you? (v 6)

5. How long will you dwell in the house of the Lord? (v 6b)

Prayer Moment: Take five minutes to rest in the quiet assurance of God's presence and love for you. Thank Him for His presence as you do so!

I love the picture of Jesus as the Good Shepherd. Jesus declares and affirms Psalm 23 that *He* is the Good Shepherd and that He lays down His life for the sheep (John 10:11). Jehovah Rohi or Yahweh Rohi is the Hebrew name which means "the Lord is my shepherd." Jesus' characteristics affirm that He is indeed our shepherd. A shepherd sets boundaries for his sheep so they do not get lost. Boundaries keep sheep from wandering aimlessly, and Jesus, the Word made flesh, gave us boundaries as He walked this earth and taught us heavenly principles.

Another trait of a shepherd is leadership. A shepherd leads by going ahead of the sheep and showing the way. Jesus is the way, the truth, and the life, and He is the example that we as sheep follow.

Jesus said in John 10:10 that He has come that we might have life and have it abundantly. When Psalm 23 says, "He makes me lie down in green pastures, this reiterates the prior verse that declares, I lack nothing." In Jesus we are filled with everything we need. In Him we can live in a place of contentment. Have you ever seen a sheep lying down in a green pasture? A green pasture is full of rich grass for grazing, and unless a sheep is completely filled and content, you will not find one lying down. It will be eating!

As I was reading about the account of Jesus feeding the five thousand (John 6), the Holy Spirit pointed out a detail in Scripture that I had never noticed before:

> [10] *Jesus said, "Have the people sit down." There was plenty of grass in that place, and they sat down (about five thousand men were there).*

Wow! Did you notice that God made it a point to mention, *there was plenty of grass*? Jesus embodied what Psalm 23 had to say about the Good Shepherd. He literally had the people, His sheep, sit down in grass.

I also find it intriguing that King David wrote about lying down in green pastures, quiet waters, a refreshed soul, walking along right paths, and then BAM!—the valley of the shadow of death. This is quite a contrast. He writes about his soul being free from agitation and then he mentions walking in the darkest valley.

Spiritually speaking, when we mention the term valley, this isn't a comfortable place to be. A *dark* valley is even worse. It is referencing death and destruction whether it refers to a relationship, a physical decline, or both. However, in faith, David casts his mind and soul toward the care of the Good Shepherd and says, **even though***...I will fear no evil, for you are with me; your rod and your staff, they comfort me.* David knows His God is faithful and will not leave him. He knows God will fight for him, even as any good shepherd fights for his sheep.

David wrote from a place of personal understanding since he was a shepherd prior to his kingship. He had experience in saving his sheep from bears and lions (1 Samuel). He knows God will deliver him from his worldly and spiritual foes as well. This is a wonderful promise for all of us to proclaim from the depths of our hearts whether we are in green grass or the darkest valley.

When I read, "your rod and your staff, they comfort me," I cannot help but think of the rod symbolizing Jesus and the staff signifying the Holy Spirit. The Hebrew word for rod is *shebet*, which suggests a scepter, or another emblem of authority.[6] Jesus states that all authority has been given to Him in heaven and on earth (Matthew 28:18). The Hebrew word for staff is *mishgneneh*, implying what a person leans upon for support.[7] The Holy Spirit guides, teaches, and helps us along our journey (John 14:26, 15:26, 16:13).

As I imagine the table Jesus has prepared for His bride, I imagine Him at the head and reclining as He often portrayed Himself when He was feasting with others. This position is a place of confidence and rest fit for the King of kings. I also envision all nine fruits of the Spirit present in their peak ripeness—love, joy, peace, patience, kindness, goodness, faithfulness, gentleness, and self-control. I also imagine the Lamb of God breaking a loaf of bread that is basted with olive oil as He pours drink fresh from His vine. Our spiritual enemies fear, pride, shame, and guilt all bow low not able to partake in the feast or attach themselves to His bride because of the anointing and protection He provides. I would love to hear how you envision His table.

In life, there are seasons of being filled to overflowing, and there are times of being poured out to emptiness. Regardless of what season you are in, you can know that the Faithful One is with you always, which will leave your soul in a state of calm and quietness. Thank Him for His goodness and lovingkindness in your life today!

[6] http://www. Biblehub.com/Hebrew   [7] Ibid

Challenge: Read Psalm 23 aloud and commit it to memory. Use it in your prayer life over yourself and your family.

I [Jesus] am the door; if anyone enters through Me, he will be saved,
and will go in and out and find pasture.
John 10:9

Notes

_____

_____

_____

_____

_____

_____

_____

_____

_____

_____

_____

_____

_____

_____

_____

_____

WEEK

Four

In him we have redemption through his blood, the forgiveness of sins,
in accordance with the riches of God's grace...
Ephesians 1:7

Redeem—to recover ownership of by paying a specified sum.[1] To buy or pay off; clear by payment.[2] Redeemed—adjective of a person granted redemption or salvation.[3]

Reading these definitions bring instant relief to my soul. To value redemption, there has to be recognition of loss. For every person, there is loss of life and lack of communion with our Father in heaven due to sin. However, because our Father is rich in kindness and mercy, we can receive redemption. Life and communion have been recovered by the One who is and always will be! **Let's read Ephesians 1:1-10.**

1. Why does Paul give blessing to God in verse three?

2. When were we chosen in Christ? (v 4)

[1] www.yourdictionary.com   [2] www.infoplease.com   [3] Lexic.us

3. In Christ, we were chosen to be what? (v 4)

4. We have redemption and the forgiveness of sins through what? (v 7)

5. When the times reach their fulfillment, what will happen? (v 10b)

You can search the whole world and never find one as giving as our Father in heaven. Redemption and adoption were bought with Jesus' blood, and now eternal life is offered freely to those who want it. Jesus' blood is precious, and He poured it out for you and me. His blood undoes every wrong decision. We have been forgiven all of our debts and purchased by the God of the universe. Redemption is sweet, reconciliation is joy, and grace is glorious.

The fact that we were called and chosen before the world was created is just another testament of God's love for us. His desire and pleasure are in us. We are lavished in His glorious treasure, Jesus Christ!

Shame, guilt, and pride—Satan's deadly tools—have no standing to steal, kill, or destroy any longer. Jesus made a spectacle of them on the cross, and we do not have to listen to these lies any longer. We can fix our eyes on Jesus any time they try to take hold of our minds and cast them back to the One who already defeated them.

There will be a time when every wrong is made right, when every crooked path is made straight, and all disease and illness vanish. What a happy day it will be once everything is brought to complete unity in heaven and on earth! Our focus shouldn't be on the culmination of time, but rather on today. Our responsibility is to build God's kingdom and reckon each task as a building block toward His great climax. Every moment has its place in history, and so do you. Knowing you have been redeemed gives you the power to walk in His righteousness and allow His refining to upgrade your life to the heights of heaven.

♥ **Are you growing closer to God and making the most of your redemption? Explain.**

Not only is this so, but we also boast in God through our Lord Jesus Christ,
through whom we have now received reconciliation.
Romans 5:11

Notes

_____

_____

_____

_____

_____

_____

I sing over you with joyful songs. I take great delight in you,
and rejoice over you with singing.
Zephaniah 3:17b

 Sing—to make musical sounds with the voice, usually a tune with words.[4]

Did you know that God sings? What an awesome and fun fact. Have you ever wondered what song God sings over you? Ask Him. He will put a tune in your heart and words that flow from your mouth. After this reading today, I imagine your heart will overflow with a melody. **Let's read the good news of Zephaniah 3:9-20.**

♥ What do you imagine *serving Him shoulder to shoulder* looks like? If you are drawing a blank, ask Him what it means for you. Then document what He says.

1. What will God do to the lips of the peoples? (v 9)

♥ What offering do you imagine you will bring to the Lord? (Teaching, healing, prayer, etc.)

2. Who will be removed from His city? (v 11)

3. Who will be left in His city? (v 12)

4. Challenge Question: According to verse thirteen, what two enemies of God will be done away with?

5. What commands are given in verse 14? Why? (v 15)

6. What promises are given in verse 17?

Reading this section of Zephaniah has encouraged my soul greatly. These are more wonderful promises to hold near as we run the race set before us. Isaiah 6 immediately flashes before my eyes as I envision the seraphim touching Isaiah's lips with a burning coal. In that account, God purified Isaiah's uncleanliness and atoned for his guilt and sin. Still, as amazing as His mercy is, the Lord immediately asked Isaiah, "Whom shall I send, and who will go for **Us**?".

Our redemption and atonement bring sweet reconciliation, but it also enables *us* to go for **Them—the Holy Trinity!** Jesus' blood atoned for our guilt and sin. Staying in His Word and applying it to each circumstance keeps us holy and blameless.

We are free to bring Him our offerings of joy, steadfastness, and love. We can have great peace, knowing that whatever offering we bring and will bring, it will be accepted and right because there will be no wrongs. As the Scripture says, *On that day...*, so we yearn for that day while seizing the moment at hand! We live out Proverbs 10:5:

> *⁵ He who gathers crops in summer is a prudent son, but*
> *he who sleeps during harvest is a disgraceful son.*

These promises encourage and catapult us to the finish line! Again, here in Zephaniah, we are told that shame has no place in us. Neither does pride or haughtiness. The meek and the humble will be left, which echoes Jesus' sermon on the Mount— "Blessed are the poor in spirit, for theirs is the kingdom of heaven", and "Blessed are the meek, for they will inherit the earth" (Matthew 5:3, 5).

And what about that singing part? I have to admit music can send me soaring to the throne room of Heaven. Another incredible account of Heaven in Jim Woodford's book states, "The flowers not only had color; they had sound as well. Accompanying the visual beauty was a concert of impromptu music created by the petals of flowers as they were moved by the constant, gentle breeze that filled the landscape." Jim asked his guardian angel, "Is that music?" He said, *"Yes, James, the flowers and all of Heaven are so happy you're here. They are filled with joy. They are singing to you."*[5] Just wow. God continues to blow me away with His awe and wonder and love. I hope this gives you a great sense of God's delight and love for you.

And did you catch the reference to Psalm 23? "They will eat and lie down and no one will make them afraid." Isn't His Word amazing? It takes you here and there, and back again. It interweaves His goodness with awesome wonder. I pray His fire in your heart is burning brighter and brighter with each eternal word that you read. We will fear no evil because fear is gone! Are you singing with rejoicing yet? Hallelujah!

The Lord will wash away the filth of the women of Zion; he will cleanse the bloodstains from Jerusalem by a spirit of judgment and a spirit of fire. Then the Lord will create over all of Mount Zion and over those who assemble there a cloud of smoke by day and a glow of flaming fire by night; over everything the glory will be a canopy.
Isaiah 4:4-5

Notes

_____

_____

_____

_____

_____

_____

_____

_____

_____

_____

_____

Let the message of Christ dwell among you richly as you teach and
admonish one another with all wisdom through psalms, hymns,
and songs from the Spirit, singing to God with gratitude in your hearts.
Colossians 3:16

Teach—to impart knowledge or skill.[6]

Regardless of what your profession is, you have taught someone something at some point. God instructs us to teach one another, specifically about Him. Jesus was the best teacher to walk this earth, and as we dig into His Word, it will teach us how to teach and be like Him. **Let's read 1 Timothy 4.**

1. What does the Spirit clearly say? (v 1)

2. Whom do these teachings come through? (v 2)

♥ **Are there superstitions that you cling to or follow? If so, what and why? Are you ready to let them go?**

3. How are we nourished? (v 6)

4. What should a good minister of Christ Jesus point out to brothers and sisters? (v 7)

5. How are we to train ourselves? (v 7)

6. What holds promise for the present life and life to come? (v 8)

7. Paul and Timothy put their hope in whom? (v 10)

8. What things are we to command and teach? (vv 12-14)

9. Why do you think you are warned not to neglect the gift that is given through prophecy and the laying on of hands? What are you supposed to do with the recognized gifts from God? (vv 14,15)

10. What will you do if you persevere in faith and godliness? (v 16)

It is alarming to know the Holy Spirit clearly says that in latter times, some believers will abandon their faith and follow deceiving spirits and things taught by demons. We are living in these days, and it is imperative to know and teach God's Word so we will not be found abandoning His kingdom. *If demons are teaching Satan's lies, how much more should we be teaching Christ's truths?*

Some of the leaders of the Ephesian church had strayed from the faith. They were following superstitions and man-made rules against eating certain foods in order to obtain salvation. They also allowed immoral behavior to enter the church. If we compare today's society to God's Word, we will see that our current culture is similar to the Ephesian church of that day. Immoral values are a pathway to death. However, a lot of churches have allowed these demons into their teachings. The world cannot define our character or the body of Christ. God's Word and Jesus' ways have to remain the rule over our individual lives and our churches.

It is by grace we are saved, through faith in Jesus Christ. Once we have surrendered our lives to Jesus, we grow in our faith by nourishing our souls with His true living Word. This need for nourishment equals the amount of time you should spend reading and meditating on the Word of God.

As we spend time in the Word, we learn what a godly life looks like, and we apply those values to our own lives. Jesus' life, as recounted in the gospels, shows us what our Father in heaven desires. Then we can teach others what He teaches us.

I do not want superstitions, bad habits, culture norms, or popular trends to define me. I want Jesus my faithful King and the fruits of His Spirit to flow freely from my heart—regardless of whatever pushback and temptation the enemy wants to throw at me. To be holy and blameless is my desire because it is what holds God's promises for my life here on earth and in my life to come.

Early on in my walk with Christ I was doing a Bible study that had the famous last words of certain people. Several of these quotations came from atheists and some from believers. The last words of the atheists were dreadful. They talked about the tormenting fire of hell. This put a holy fear of God in my heart.

At that time in my life, I had a problem with using profanity. I noticed that I would generally say these curses when I was driving and fear would overcome me. A car might cut in front of me, and, fearful of a wreck, I would say these bad words. One night, I confessed this to the leaders of the Bible study because I was afraid to die with these last words on my lips. It was at that moment of confession and humility that I believe God's grace delivered me from cursing, and His fire from heaven purified my speech.

Another part of growing in Jesus is realizing and accomplishing the tasks He has prepared in advance for us. We do this by using the special gifts God knit into our hearts. Some of the gifts we receive are given in impartation from prophets of God. Paul teaches us a lot about prophesy and urges every one of us to prophesy (1 Cor. 14).

In this letter to Timothy, Paul continues to encourage us regarding prophecy from the Lord. When a trusted man of God and prophet lays hands on you and imparts heavenly gifts, we should receive this present from God and put the talent to use.

Otherwise, we hinder our own faith, as well as those who were witnesses to the prophecy. Faith and action go hand in hand. James gives us a great illustration of faith and action regarding Abraham's life. Abraham was considered righteous for what he did when he offered his son Isaac on the altar. We see that Abraham's faith and actions worked together, and his faith was made complete by what he did (James 2:20-22).

Pray for boldness, courage, and obedience to step into what God has called you to, and watch Jesus author new levels of faith into your spirit! As you become a doer of God's Word, your life will be a testimony of God's faithfulness that spreads like wildfire.

I have had the privilege and honor of receiving impartation from trusted prophets of God, and it is life-changing. Usually they confirm what God has already spoken to your heart, because His Word has been knit into your heart before creation existed. Sometimes they can illuminate possibilities you may have never considered. God may want to draw attention to something He has been trying to tell you, but you may have not been listening. As we pray about it, our spirit bears witness.

If we choose to disregard the Father's words, we may hinder both us and our witnesses. This would be like water being poured over an emerging fire. Our faith and the faith of others would smolder. So be diligent in what the Lord prompts you to do, so He can move you from one level of glory to the next and His holy fire will blaze upon you and fellow believers (2 Cor. 3:18).

For this reason I remind you to fan into flame the gift of God,
which is in you through the laying on of my hands. For the Spirit God gave
us does not make us timid, but gives us power, love, and self-discipline.
2 Timothy 1:6-7

Notes

_____

_____

_____

_____

_____

_____

_____

_____

_____

_____

_____

_____

_____

_____

_____

And we all, who with unveiled faces contemplate the Lord's glory,
are being transformed into his image with ever-increasing glory,
which comes from the Lord, who is the Spirit.
2 Corinthians 3:18

U Unveiled—disclosed; revealed;
to remove a veil or covering from.[7]

I am overflowing with joy because the Holy Spirit is enabling me to write fluidly.
I am amazed at how He lined up these days for study. Did you notice how we ended
Day 3 with reference to 2 Cor. 3:18 and are starting today with the same verse? God
is so attentive and orderly! I did not plan these writings, but His Holy Spirit has
guided me, and He is teaching us all. **Let's read 2 Corinthians 3:7-18 as well
as Exodus 34:29-35 and continue to be taught in the Lord.**

Exodus:

1. When Moses came down from Mount Sinai, what was different? (v 29)

2. Was Moses aware of this change?

3. Why was Moses' face radiant? (v 29)

4. How did Aaron and the Israelites respond to Moses' radiance? (v 30)

5. When would Moses put the veil on? (v 33)

6. When would Moses take the veil off? (v 34)

Can you imagine being so immersed in the presence of the Lord, your face becomes radiant with His glory? Moses' face absorbed the magnificent eternal light and life from our Creator. This was an answered request from the Lord to Moses (Exodus 33) when Moses asked the Lord to show him His glory. The Lord did this because He was pleased with Moses and because He knew Moses by name (33:17). I wonder how long it would take for God's manifest glory to fade when Moses was away from His presence. How long did Moses have to wear a veil so that the Israelite community would not be in fear?

7. Why do you think the Israelites, including Aaron, were in fear? Take some time and write your thoughts and revelations below.

I love the picture of Moses speaking to the Lord without the veil. It is such a beautiful foreshadowing of the new covenant with Jesus, our Savior, and how we can now directly approach our Father. We can enter into His presence because of Jesus' shed blood and resurrection. Jesus' blood prepares us and sanctifies us from all unrighteousness, so we can boldly enter into His throne room and rise and shine His glory!

We do not have to put a veil on after being in His presence. The world may not recognize Jesus' light, and some will despise it (John 15:18), but we are not to put it under a basket. Rather, we are to shine Him unabashedly like a lamp displayed on a lampstand.

2 Corinthians 3:7-18:

8. What did the first ministry (law) bring? (v 7)

9. What does the ministry of the Spirit (Jesus' death and resurrection) bring? (v 9)

10. How long does the glory of the new covenant last? (v 11)

11. With eternal glory as our hope, how are we to act? (v 12)

12. In what state are the minds of those who do not know Christ? (v 14a)

13. The veil still remains on some, but is taken away only in who? (v 14)

14. When Moses is read, the veil covers what part of the body? (v 15)

15. When is the veil taken away? (v 16)

16. What is found in the Spirit of the Lord? (v 17)

♥ What does freedom look like to you?

17. How are we being transformed according to verse eighteen?

Are you very bold? This is not a suggestion. Paul commands Timothy to walk in boldness, "For God did not give us a spirit of timidity, but a spirit of power, of love and self-discipline" (2 Timothy 1:7). There is freedom in the Spirit, and even when faced with intimidation and false accusations, we can walk in the power of Almighty God because of our eternal covenant with Him. His glory is ever-increasing and testifies to Jesus' righteousness and resurrection life.

I have the Lord's compassion for the lost. With a veil covering their heart, it is no wonder their minds are dull. Proverbs 4:23 says, "Above all else, guard your heart, for everything you do flows from it." *Jesus, guard our hearts in You and remove the veil from the hearts of the lost!*

Both gospels, Matthew and Mark, give us details on the temple curtain being torn when Jesus gave up His Spirit. Here is what Matthew 27:50-52 depicts:

> *[50] And when Jesus had cried out again in a loud voice, he gave up his spirit.*
> *[51] At that moment the curtain of the temple was torn in two from top to bottom.*
> *The earth shook, the rocks split [52] and the tombs broke open.*

Wow! At the very moment that Jesus gave up His spirit, the thick fabric wall that separated man from God was destroyed. As *soon* as anyone turns to the Lord, the veil is removed from his heart! Only in Christ is the veil that covers our hearts and dulls our minds split in two. There is no longer anything separating us from the presence of our Father. The day Jesus gave up His life for the world, the thick curtain split from *top* to *bottom* so no man could claim that power. Only Jesus.

It is only in King Jesus that we find freedom. He is the exact location of freedom. If you typed *freedom* in a GPS device, Jesus would be the one and only destination. As soon as you turn towards Him, you have arrived! The good news is, He isn't far off.

Freedom isn't a ticket to sin. Rather it is the blessing and green light to be who you are in Christ. Psalm 118:19-21 says:

> [19]*Open for me the gates of the righteous; I will enter and give thanks to the Lord.*
> [20]*This is the gate of the Lord through which the righteous may enter.* [21]*I will give you thanks, for You answered me; you have become my salvation.*

Once you have accepted Jesus as your salvation, you can enter into the gates of heaven and find freedom, joy, and the best life! Call and turn to Him while He may be found.

So if the Son sets you free, you will be free indeed.
John 8:36

Notes

_____

_____

_____

_____

_____

_____

_____

The sting of death is sin, and the power of sin is the law. But thanks be to God! He gives us the victory through our Lord Jesus Christ.
1 Corinthians 15:56-57

𝒱. Victorious—conquering; triumphant; having conquered in any conquest or in battle; having overcome an antagonist or enemy.[8]

We are victorious through our Lord Jesus Christ. Praise God.
Let's read Isaiah 25:1-9.

Praise God out loud and list at least five things that God has done on your behalf. What miracles have you seen Him do? Ask Him to bring them to mind if you cannot think of any. They are all around!

♥

♥

♥

♥

♥

1. What has God done to the city and fortified town? (v 2)

2. What will this action cause strong people and ruthless nations to do? (v 3)

3. God is a refuge for whom? (v 4)

4. Ultimately, what will the Lord do on the mountain? (v 8)

5. What will the people say of God? (v 9)

God has brought the verse Mark 10:27 to my attention repeatedly in the last few weeks. It says, "Jesus looked at them and said, "With man this is impossible, but not with God; all things are possible with God." As I read Isaiah 25, I can see God fulfilling this very scripture. It starts off by praising God for doing miraculous things! Continuing in verse two, God does something that is unimaginable. He makes a city into a heap of trash and brings a fortified city to ruin.

I picture a city full of people hustling and bustling about. Everything needed is within close proximity. There are malls, grocery stores, gas stations, and hospitals all within a short distance of one another. A fortified city is strong and secure with some sort of stone wall or iron gate around it. Yet we read that God brought the fortified city to ruin so it could never be rebuilt.

In this humbling act, God causes the prideful, strong, and violent nations to fear and revere the One true God. For the meek, helpless, and weak, God becomes a refuge and a shelter from the storm. As a cloud instantly brings relief from the blazing sun, the Lord silences the mockery of arrogant tyrants. There is an immediate physical relief from oppression.

As we continue reading, it keeps getting better. Upon the mountain, the mountain of Jesus, God Almighty prepares a lavish feast with the choicest of foods and drink. Does this bring Psalm 23 to mind again? He prepares a feast in the presence of our enemies! Yet, on the mountain, the enemy of death is swallowed and defeated forever. On this mountain, the mountain of Jesus, He will destroy the hindrances that keep people from seeing Him. He will remove the veil that dulls their minds and hardens their hearts.

My heart is so tender towards our loving, living, and amazing God as I think about His goodness. I want to share an amazing testimony of a miracle God performed in my life. I believe it will encourage you.

The Lord woke me in the early morning August 7, 2021, and put a specific friend and her children on my heart, so I started to pray for them all. I had been thinking about her all week and had meant to reach out but had not. We lived four hours away from each other, and would have had to make special plans to meet—or so I thought.

On this particular day, we were coming home from our working ranch in West Texas via I-10. Although we needed gas, we had passed our usual fill-up station. We thought we would just take the next exit, but soon saw we had already passed it too. Fortunately, we had enough gas. So we continued.

Not too many miles down the road, my husband, Rob, saw the friend I had prayed for merging onto the highway! I quickly called her and asked if she was on I-10. When she answered, I could hear her weeping.

We both pulled over at the next exit and embraced each other with hugs from heaven, amazed at how God had brought us together. When she saw my name pop up on her phone, she had said, "This is impossible!" She had been weeping with sorrow for days because her son had reached a state of hopelessness and despair. He believed the lies of the enemy and felt himself a failure, to the extent he called her and threatened to take his life. Since they lived in different countries, it was impossible for her to check on him.

My friend wanted to reach out to me, for she knew I would pray, but she had hesitated. Isn't our living and compassionate God so amazing? God was close to her and her broken heart. In that closeness, He woke me up to intercede on her behalf. Then, in His perfect timing and leading, He arranged for us to "accidentally" meet on His righteous highway.

He makes the impossible possible. What an encouragement and leap in faith this was for us both! Thank You, Jesus, for authoring our faith to a higher level that day in August.

My friend and I laughed and rejoiced that God had had this event on His calendar before creation existed! He executed His wonderful plan through His faithfulness and loving kindness. I know God is revealing Himself to her son, and He is removing the thoughts of death from his heart.

Prayer:

Father, we thank You, that You are alive and active and present in our life and in our circumstances. You are close to the brokenhearted, and You are moving in all of our lives right now. Let us be obedient to Your ways right now and forevermore. Lead us on Your righteous paths for Your namesake. Take away the spirit of hopelessness and despair and give us all the full measure of Your hope, faith, and love. Let those who feel helpless hear Your loving voice as You destroy the strongholds in their minds. Let the mountain of Jesus be where they run to for refuge and security. Do the impossible so Your name is glorified. We are victorious through You, Jesus, our Lord and Savior. Your blood speaks a better word . . . it shouts life and VICTORY! Amen.

'He will wipe every tear from their eyes. There will be no more death' or mourning
or crying or pain, for the old order of things has passed away.
Revelation 21:4

Notes

_____

_____

_____

_____

_____

WEEK

Five

Day 1

and the blood of Jesus, his Son, purifies us from all sin.
1 John 1:7b

W. Washed—to cleanse, using water
or other liquid.[1]

Depending on what we use to clean and wash with, we could have different levels
of cleanliness. In the store, we can find all sorts of detergents, stain removers, spot
treatments, and natural remedies that claim to remove the toughest stains. Although
we like to have clean and stain-free clothes, the Bible talks about another type
of stain. **Let's read 1 John 1 and see what God says about being purified
and cleansed.**

1. To what does the author (most likely Apostle John) of this letter testify? (vv 1, 2)

2. Is darkness found in God? (v 5)

3. How do we know if we are living out His truth? (v 6)

[1] www.thefreedictionary.com

4. What does a life walking in the light look like?

5. What does a life in the light guarantee? (v 7)

6. What happens when we confess our sins? (v 9)

I vividly remember the day I asked Jesus into my heart. The summer of 1993, I went to Rainbow River Christian camp with my brother and cousins. I was nine years old, and I still remember the sermon that I heard and the powerful demonstration the pastor gave.

He used two cups of liquid—one was black, representing our sinful hearts, and the other was red, representing the blood of Jesus. The speaker explained our sinful nature and how no one was born without sin, except Jesus, the Son of God. The pastor led us through scripture that spoke about Jesus' sinless life and explained Jesus' crucifixion and how His blood cleansed our sinful hearts if we believed in our hearts and confessed with our mouths. He then proceeded to pour the red liquid into the cup of black liquid. In an instant, it became clear!

I was overwhelmed by the Holy Spirit and moved to repentance because I knew my heart had the stain of many sins, even at the age of nine. I knew I needed the blood of Jesus to cleanse my heart as white as snow.

John and the other disciples testified to what their eyes had seen and their hands had touched. They saw Jesus, the Son of God, walked beside Him, and touched Him. They were so bold in their testimonies because they had first-person accounts of who He was and is. They witnessed that there is no darkness in God. He cannot lie or sin.

The disciples painstakingly witnessed Jesus pour out His blood so that the penalty of sin was met. When God triumphantly raised Jesus from the dead, He enabled the new covenant for us to remain pure and holy. Jesus' blood is the only way to cleanse our hearts from sin completely and perfectly. We walk in Jesus' light which is His love, and we do not practice sinning as we once did. We are purified and made righteous through His faithfulness and justice.

If we confess our sins, he is faithful and just and will forgive
us our sins and purify us from all unrighteousness.
1 John 1:9

Notes

_____

_____

_____

_____

_____

_____

_____

_____

So God created mankind in his own image, in the image of God
he created them; male and female he created them.
Genesis 1:27

 Xeroxed—a photocopy, copy, reproduction, or duplicate.[2]

When I was writing The ABCs of God's Promises, the Holy Spirit immediately dropped *Xeroxed* in my heart for the letter X. If you've ever played an ABC game where you have to come up with something that starts with the letter X, you may find it difficult. I typically think of xylophone or X-ray. However, our loving Father didn't skip a beat when He spoke to me for this love letter. His hand in our creation is undeniable. Let's go back to the beginning as we draw near to the end of this study. **Read Genesis 1:26-31.**

1. Challenge Question: Who do you think "Us" represents in verse 26?

2. How did God create mankind? (v 27)

3. What did God do to mankind before speaking to them? (v 28)

♥ Have you received a blessing lately? If so, describe.

4. What commands did God give mankind? (v 28)

5. What did God give mankind and why? (v 29)

6. Did God make provision for the animals? (v 30)

7. Looking at all that God had made, what did He think about it all? (v 31)

I love reading Genesis, because we get access to God's conversations and reasoning regarding creation and the beginning of time as we know it. We actually gain access to the Holy Trinity's conversation regarding *us*, mankind! Can you imagine the Three in One speaking about your creation and how *you* would mirror *Their* image spiritually? We were created in the image of the Father, Son, and Holy Spirit!

Isaiah 11:2-4ab is a great reference to the image of our triune God:

> [2] *The Spirit of the LORD will rest on him [Jesus]—the Spirit of wisdom and of understanding, the Spirit of counsel and of might, the Spirit of the knowledge and fear of the LORD–and he will delight in the fear of the LORD. He will not judge by what he sees with his eyes, or decide by what he hears with his ears; but with righteousness he will judge the needy, with justice he will give decisions for the poor of the earth.*

This passage reveals God and His attributes in seven spirits—The Spirit of the Lord, the Spirit of wisdom, the Spirit of understanding, the Spirit of counsel, the Spirit of strength, the Spirit of knowledge, and the Spirit of fear of the Lord. In Jesus, we see the fullness of His seven Spirits.

These verses specifically speak about Jesus as the awaited Messiah and chosen one that Israel was waiting for, but it also gives us as children of God the revelation of who we are in Him. Made in the Triune image of God, we have access and permission to God's fullness. These seven spirits equip us to rule and reign, even as they equipped and empowered Jesus.

In creating us in His image and likeness, God also made a distinction between mankind in creating male and female. In His process of creating man and woman, He made differences. Adam was made from the dust, and Eve was made from Adam's rib (Gen. 2:7, 2:21-22). The Holy Trinity was intentional in His differing designs and functions for the two sexes.

As male and female become one in holy marriage (Gen. 2:23-25), they are able to obey His command and be fruitful and increase. God never meant for mankind to change their genders or confuse their roles. God detests this and is clear on the fate of those who do (Lev. 20:13, Deut. 22:5, 1 Cor. 6:18).

Jesus also reiterates God's intention for man and woman saying, "Haven't you read,"

He replied, "that at the beginning the Creator made them male and female, and said, 'For this reason a man will leave his father and mother and be united to his wife, and the two will become one flesh?' So they are no longer two, but one flesh. Therefore what God has joined together, let no one separate" (Matthew 19:4-6).

After God created man in His image, male and female, He blessed them. He immediately gave them the ability to walk in the Spirit of the Lord and the spirits of wisdom, counsel, strength, understanding, knowledge, and fear of the Lord, so they could accomplish all that God commanded. The first mandates the Lord gave Adam and Eve were to fill the earth with children and rule and reign over creation. God specifically instructed mankind to rule over the fish, birds, and every living creature that moves on the ground. He provided food to nourish men, women, and beast. There wasn't a need that wasn't met. He is so generous and kind-hearted.

The fact that God cares for all of His creation is especially endearing to my heart. Are you an animal lover or know somebody who is? My husband is a rancher who raises animals and a farmer who harvests vegetation for food. Jesus blessed him with the desire to raise exotic African animals. The wisdom and knowledge required to care for these beasts is incredible.

Part of ruling over different species of animals is knowing what plants they eat and the type of environment in which they thrive. Choosing the precise grass seed, planting and harvesting at the correct time, and settling animals in the correct topography and climate is vital for success. God graciously gives people discernment for managing these creatures, big and small, if they seek Him to fulfill the Genesis mandate. Although the fall of sin made working the land a more difficult task, it must be done, and we have success if we honor and seek the Lord.

Recently God has given me a keen awareness for ranchers and farmers all over the world. Not long ago I noticed that the bag of cashews I was eating was harvested in a Latin American country. I prayed that the Lord would bless the harvesters and farmers and they would come to know Jesus as their Savior.

After creation was set and finished, God saw all that He had done and recognized it as *very good*. He didn't have second thoughts to what, who, or how He spoke things into existence. The Ancient of Days saw everything before Him, and He was delighted enough to stop creating and rest (Genesis 2:2).

♥ **When you complete a task the Lord has given you, do you find it easy or difficult to rest in the work that was completed? Why or why not?**

Let's bless the Lord and thank Him for creating us in His image!

Prayer:

Holy Trinity, we thank You for creating us in Your image. No other creatures were given the fullness of Your Spirit. Thank You for giving us authority over all creation and teaching us how to establish Your kingdom here on earth. You are so caring and generous, and we praise Your Holy name! Thank You for pouring out the Spirit of the Lord upon us, the Spirit of wisdom, the Spirit of understanding, the Spirit of counsel, the Spirit of might, the Spirit of the knowledge, and the Spirit of fear of the Lord. Let us rule in Your righteousness and faithfulness!

> *The righteous will inherit the land and dwell in it forever.*
> *The mouth of the righteous utters wisdom, and his tongue speaks justice.*
> *The law of His God is in his heart; His steps do not slip.*
> *Psalms 37:29-31*

Notes

_____

_____

_____

_____

_____

_____

_____

_____

_____

_____

_____

_____

_____

_____

_____

He gives strength to the weary and increases the power of the weak.

Isaiah 40:29

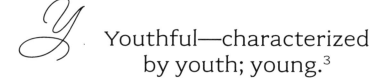 Youthful—characterized
by youth; young.[3]

I had breakfast with my slightly older friend the other morning, and we were talking about how we feel younger than our calendar ages. This is a trait He has given especially to those who are born-again believers. One of my husband's favorite scriptures is 2 Peter 3:8, "But do not forget this one thing, dear friends: With the Lord a day is like a thousand years, and a thousand years are like a day." What an awesome, wonderful promise! **Let's read Isaiah 40:28-31.**

1. What age/timeline is given to God? (v 28)

2. Does God grow tired or weary?

♥ **Have you ever found yourself growing weary or weak? If so, describe.**

3. What does God do for the weary and weak? (v 29)

4. What promise is given to those who hope in the Lord? (v 31)

I have mentioned before that Isaiah is one of my favorite books in the Bible. In its beautiful words, I find comfort and hope. God doesn't grow old, weary, or tired. He is the one and only everlasting God. Time is in His hands, as Job 12:10 says, "In his hand is the life of every creature and the breath of all mankind."

As a mom, I can feel weariness some days more than others. I remember being especially tired when my three daughters were toddlers. I thought a full night's sleep would never come! I would have a 3 p.m. coffee regularly in those days to give me energy to finish my day. Yet, God in His true fashion, has taken my weariness away and given me more strength than I could imagine. A dear friend gave me a bracelet that says "STRONG." I love it because it reminds me my strength comes from Him. I expect His supernatural strength, especially on the days when I feel less than one hundred percent.

Still, those who hope in the Lord have a marvelous promise. When we find ourselves in circumstances that look dire and impossible, God is just a prayer away with new strength and refreshing, mighty winds to take us to heights our minds have not imagined.

The image and characteristics of an eagle are brilliant. God made eagles to dwell in high places. You do not find their homes in low trees, but rather atop high cliffs and mountains. Their vision is extraordinary, with eyesight estimated at four to eight times stronger than an average human. When they spot their prey, they leap off of the high places and *soar*. Their wings are so powerful and large that if they were to flap their wings vigorously instead of soaring with them outstretched, they would snap their necks!

Just like the eagles, we are not created to dwell in low places. We are seated in the heavenly places with Christ, and we soar in His strength vs. striving in our limited neck-snapping strength. We keep our eyes locked on the prize of Jesus as we run the race set before us. We will walk and not be faint. We will endure whatever trials are before us and hope for the things not yet seen. In the hope of the Lord, we will never be put to shame. Be encouraged whatever your season or calendar age, because renewed strength is your promise!

The blameless spend their days under the Lord's care,
and their inheritance will endure forever.
Psalm 37:18

Notes

_____

_____

_____

_____

_____

_____

_____

_____

Day 4

Never be lacking in zeal, but keep your spiritual fervor, serving the Lord.

Romans 12:11

 Zealous—marked by fervent partisanship for a person, a cause, or an ideal: filled with or characterized by zeal.[4]

A few synonyms for zealous are enthusiastic, passionate, and earnest. The Bible instructs us to be zealous and sold out for Christ and His ways. As we approach our last two days of the study, **let's read Revelation 3:14-22**, and see exactly what Jesus says in regard to our devotion towards our Father and His kingdom.

1. To what city did the angel of the church write? (v 14)

2. In verse fourteen, what three names are given Jesus?

3. What does Jesus know? (v 15)

[4] www.merriam-webster.com

4. What will Jesus do to the lukewarm? (v 16)

5. What do the Laodiceans think about themselves? (v 17)

6. What is their spiritual state in reality? (v 17b)

7. What counsel does Jesus give? What do you think this symbolizes? (v 18)

8. What does Jesus do to those He loves? (v 19)

9. What two commands does Jesus give in verse 19b?

10. Challenge Question: What do you think verse 20 means?

11. What is promised to the one who is victorious?

Can you imagine scribing the very words of The Amen, The Faithful and True Witness, and The Beginning of the Creation of God? This is who we serve! Our living God, sees, hears, and knows all that was, is, and is to come and He reveals these mysteries to His children. The last book of the Bible is named Revelation, which means *unveiling*. The Holy Spirit guided the disciple John as he wrote this book to reveal the nature of the Lamb, King Jesus, and to help prepare the end-times generation. Jesus also addresses some issues with believers in the Laodicean church at that time. The believers had lost their zeal for God's kingdom and instead took comfort in material things. This caused them to receive the title *lukewarm*.

In this study, we will focus on the instruction to the church in Laodicea (present day Turkey), which was a prosperous city about forty miles south of Philadelphia (note AMP).

To give you some context about this specific city, it is interesting to know Laodicea had a thriving financial system, specifically in the black wool textile production. This city was also known for a medical school that produced a sought-after eye salve.

The cares and luxuries of the world stole the hearts of the Laodiceans. The believers had no loyalty and passion for Jesus, and this made Him want to vomit them out of His mouth. This is an intense statement, because spitting/vomiting is done with force to remove bad or spoiled contents. The Laodiceans found their well-being and security in the wealth of the world, while forsaking the truth and eternal riches. Their temporary comfort blinded them to the reality of their spiritual weakness, short-sightedness, and nakedness, so Jesus wanted to address this and direct His loved ones back to Him.

We are able to receive eternal gold in heaven through the sacrifice of Jesus. He was tested like gold and put through the fiery furnace of hell, where He was proven faithful as He made a spectacle of the enemy. When Shadrach, Meshach, and Abednego were thrown into the furnace of blazing fire, they were neither burned nor did they have any effect of a fire on their bodies, hair, or robes (Daniel 3:27). Like them, Jesus was not touched by the fires of hell. Jesus made a proclamation to the spirits in prison and humiliated Satan (1 Peter 3:19, Colossians 2:15). Hallelujah!

Jesus was resurrected and clothed in white fine linen, representing His purity and perfection, which He will clothe His bride in as well. Our healing was earned by Jesus when He endured the thirty-nine lashes across His back before going to the cross. It is by His stripes that we ARE healed. When we accept Jesus as Lord and Savior, we are a new creation; old things have passed away, all things are made new (2 Cor. 5:17). Our spiritual eyes and ears are open to see and hear truth when we open our hearts to Him. You may recall the day you gave your life to Christ and how everything literally looked brand new. A friend of mine proclaimed Jesus as Lord on New Year's Eve, and the following day the world looked different. For the first time, she noticed the leaves on the trees outside her window and heard the beautiful chirping of the birds. It is truly remarkable!

The Laodiceans were known for a highly favored eye salve but they took their eyes off of Jesus. Putting their hope in this remedy alone would end in disappointment because it would eventually run out. Perhaps some recipients might have had adverse side effects. Maybe it cured eye problems with no problems, but my point is, Jesus is the one true eternal hope for all, and in Him no one is put to shame.

Jesus lovingly reproved His flock so they could repent and share the gospel of the true and faithful Witness, Jesus Christ. It is in Him that we are refined to perfection so that as we go through the fire with Him, we are not burned up like chaff. It is by His blood that we are made pure and covered in white linen, the heavenly wardrobe. It is in Jesus we are given spiritual eyes to see and ears to hear.

Jesus makes Himself known and knocks on all hearts of mankind. He says that He wants all people to be saved and to come to a knowledge of the truth (1 Timothy 2:4). Whoever hears Jesus' voice and opens the door of their heart to Him, will be saved. We are made to be a kingdom and priests to serve our Father and God. These victorious ones will have a seat on the throne of Jesus. Praise to the Father, the Son, and the Holy Spirit. Let's pray.

Prayer:

Heavenly Father, the words of Your Son are true because He is Truth. You discipline those You love, so we may be found worthy and victorious through Jesus—the living One! I ask that Your fire would be put in our hearts so we would burn for You and Your kingdom. Let our hearts and lives be the timber required to keep Your fire and zeal burning. Let our feet be resilient like Jesus' burnished bronze feet so we will not turn from the cup You have given us, and let our clothes be as white as snow, that we would be found holy and blameless in Jesus. I ask that You pour out Your grace and mercy upon us as we serve You with passion. Amen.

To Him who loves us and released us from our sins by His blood—
and He has made us to be a kingdom, priests to His God and Father—
to Him be the glory and dominion forever and ever. Amen.
Revelation 1:5b-6 NASB

Notes

_____

_____

_____

_____

_____

_____

_____

_____

_____

_____

_____

_____

_____

_____

Day 5

"Behold, I am coming quickly, and My reward is with Me, to render
to every man according to what he has done. I am the Alpha and the Omega,
the first and the last, the beginning and the end."
Revelation 21:12-13 NASB

The End. Well my friend, we have reached the final day!

I do pray that throughout these past five weeks, His promises and truths have taken root in your heart. His Word is alive and active, doing a good and eternal work—even today! I have found that when I read the Bible, the Lord always puts a person in my path with whom I can share His Word. It is exhilarating to walk in His truth and speak His life into others. I encourage you to share His eternal Word with someone today. This is one way to fulfill the commandment to love others as yourself.

As we come to the close of this study, I find it fitting to end on Jesus' last words, "Yes, I am coming quickly." Heaven's time is different than our twenty-four-hour earthly rotation, so we need to number our days and live as if He is coming today.

I would like to end this study with some practical questions to help prepare our hearts for the return of the King of kings. Ask the Holy Spirit to guide your heart into truth, so you are not deceived like the Laodiceans. These questions are not meant to bring condemnation, so do not let guilt or shame in your heart. There is only room for His truth.

⁴www.merriam-webster.com

1. Have you accepted Jesus as your Lord and Savior? If so, share the testimony! If not, do not let another second go by without Him as your Lord. Commit your life to Jesus now. If you received Jesus' salvation today, please speak to your Bible study leader and email me, Heather@Jesusishealer.com

2. If you knew Jesus was coming back today, what would your life look like? Who would you share the news with?

3. If you notice characteristics that go against the fruit of the Spirit, are you quick to ask for forgiveness and repent?

4. Noah prepared the ark for a flood, and when he was 600 years old, the flood waters came. Noah may not have understood the full picture of God's plan, but he was still obedient to the task given to him (Genesis 6-9). What tasks/gift has the Lord given you? Have you put it into practice? If so, explain. If not, how can you start?

Go out and be His love and light! Teach one another His Word as you sing songs of praise and thanksgiving to His holy name. Let your life be the timber required for the fire of Jesus to burn continually. The Holy Spirit will remind you of His words as He guides you into truth. Do not be afraid. You are the adored, beloved, and chosen daughter of the Most High King!

The Spirit and the bride say, "Come." And let the one who hears say, "Come."
And let the one who is thirsty come; let the one who wishes take the water of life without cost.
Revelation 22:17 NASB

Notes

ANSWER INDEX

Day 1

1. Arise & shine.
2. Your light has come and the glory of the Lord rises upon you.
3. The Lord rises upon you and His glory appears over you.
4. All assemble and come to you.
5. Splendor.
6. 44 (the exact number is not the goal; rather understanding these promises are for YOU).
7. Various answers.

Day 2

1. Compassion, kindness, humility, gentleness, patience.
2. Both are commands.
3. Love.
4. We are members of one body called to peace.
5. Belt of truth.
6. Breastplate of righteousness.
7. With the readiness that comes from the gospel of peace.
8. Extinguishes all the flaming arrows of the evil one.
9. We are to pray in the Spirit on all occasions—with all kinds of prayers and requests for the Lord's people.

Day 3

1. So we may have the full measure of Jesus' joy within us.
2. No. We are set apart in Christ (May be more various answers).
3. Jesus.
4. Through Jesus' sanctification.
5. Me & you— those who trust in Him.
6. All who will believe in Jesus.
7. That we would be one with our Father as Jesus is One with Him and that the world would believe our Father sent Jesus.
8. The glory that our Heavenly Father gave Jesus—The glory Jesus gives us.
9. The world will know that God sent Jesus and that we have been loved with the same love that God had for Jesus.

10. Some people reject God's love and truth for their lives.
11. The Father, so that His love would be in us.
12. God's love and Jesus, Himself.

Day 4

1. She learned Jesus was there. Note: She learned and acted!
2. Alabaster jar of perfume.
3. Various answers. Genuine repentance, desire for truth, forgiveness, vulnerability, worship, and holiness.
4. Symbol of adoration, respect, genuine love, humility, and moved by true worship in Spirit and truth (John 4:24).
5. Contempt, disdain, judgement.
6. He answered him with a parable.
7. Water for Jesus' feet, greet with a holy kiss, and oil upon His head.
8. Wet His feet with her tears, kissed His feet, poured perfume on His feet.
9. Her many sins have been forgiven.
10. Your sins are forgiven, Your faith has saved you, go in peace.

Day 5

1. A prisoner for the Lord.
2. A life worthy of the calling we have received.
3. In humility, gentleness, patience, and bearing with one another in love.
4. Through the bond of peace.
5. One body, One Spirit, One hope, One Lord, One faith, One baptism, and One God (all roads do not lead to God— there is One Way, Jesus Christ).
6. To each one.

WEEK TWO

Day 1

1. Alert and fully sober.
2. Obedient children.
3. Ignorance.
4. In ALL we do.
5. God is holy.
6. The empty way of life handed down to us from our ancestors.
7. The precious blood of Christ.
8. My sake and your sake.
9. Obeying the truth.
10. Sincere love.
11. Living and enduring Word of God.

Day 2

1. No.
2. Sets you free from law of sin and death.
3. The righteous requirement of the law might be fully met in us— so we live according to the Spirit and not out of our flesh.
4. Life and peace.
5. Life because of His righteousness.
6. Children of God.
7. His glory.
8. The glory that will be revealed in us.
9. The freedom and glory of the Children of God.
10. In all things, God works for the good.
11. Predestined to be conformed to the image of Jesus and He also called, justified, and glorified us.
12. No one.
13. No one.
14. Christ Jesus.

Day 3

1. Jesus—True Vine; God our Father—Gardener.
2. Cuts off every branch in Jesus that does not bear fruit and prunes branches that do bear fruit so they will be even more fruitful.
3. Remain in Jesus.
4. Branches.
5. They are thrown away into the fire and burned (do not enter Heaven).
6. Ask Jesus whatever we wish and it will be done for us. Our Heavenly Father receives the glory.
7. Keeping Jesus' commands.
8. Keeping His commands and remaining in His love just like Jesus kept God's commands.

Day 4

1. Grace and peace in abundance
2. Goodness, knowledge, self-control, perseverance, godliness, mutual affection, love.
3. Nearsighted and blind.
4. You will never stumble and you will receive a rich welcome into the eternal kingdom of our Lord and Savior Jesus Christ.

Day 5

1. So that everyone who believes may have eternal life.
2. God so loved the world.
3. Condemned.
4. Everyone who does evil— they are afraid their deeds will be exposed (shame and guilt).
5. Various answers.
6. Various answers.
7. Various answers.

Day 1

1. He has searched me.
2. Before a word is on my tongue.
3. Various answers.
4. Everywhere— the heavens, the depths, wings of the dawn, the far side of the sea, and darkness which is light to Him.
5. God.
6. Fearfully and wonderfully.
7. A vast (enormous) amount; too many to count.

Day 2

1. Justice.
2. In faithfulness.
3. He stretches out the heavens, spreads out the earth with all that springs from it, gives breath and life to its people.
4. Righteousness.
5. Various possible answers. He will take hold of my hand, He will keep me and will make me a covenant for the people, and He will free captives from prison.
6. He announces them to me.
7. Sing to the Lord a new song from the ends of the earth.
8. The Lord will march out like a champion, like a warrior He will stir up His zeal, with a shout He will raise the battle cry and will triumph over His enemies.
9. He leads the blind by ways they have not known (righteous paths). He guides them and turns darkness into light before them. Various personal answers.
10. They will be turned back in utter shame.

Day 3

1. Jesus.
2. Living stones.
3. A spiritual house to be a holy priesthood, offering spiritual sacrifices acceptable to God through Jesus Christ.
4. No. Never.
5. Precious.
6. The Cornerstone that causes people to stumble and a rock that makes them to fall.
7. To disobey His message.

Day 4

1. Do not fear because He has redeemed me and He summons me by name; I am His.
2. When I pass through waters.
3. I will not be burned and the flames will not set me ablaze.
4. Egypt and Seba.
5. Because I am precious and honored in His sight and because He loves me.
6. Do not be afraid.
7. For God's glory.

Day 5

1. My Shepherd.
2. The Lord, Jesus, is my guide and protector. I lack nothing.
3. Sheep lying down in green pastures means they are full/content. They cannot eat the ripe grass because they are filled with His goodness. I have everything in Jesus.
4. All the days of my life.
5. Forever.

WEEK 4

Day 1
1. He is the God and Father of our Lord Jesus who has blessed us in the heavenly realms with every spiritual blessing in Christ.
2. Before the creation of the world.
3. Holy & blameless.
4. Jesus' blood.
5. All things will be brought to unity in heaven and on earth under Christ.

Day 2
1. Purify the lips that all of them may call on the name of the Lord.
2. Arrogant boasters.
3. The meek & humble.
4. The spirit of lies/deceit, and spirit of fear.
5. Sing, shout aloud, be glad and rejoice with all your heart because the Lord has taken away your punish ment and has turned back my enemy– the Lord is with me and I will never fear harm again.
6. The Lord my God is with me. He will take great delight in me. He will no longer rebuke me. He will rejoice over me with singing.

Day 3
1. In later times some will abandon the faith and follow deceiving spirits and things taught by demons.
2. Hypocritical liars whose consciences have been seared as with a hot iron.
3. Point out God's truths. We are nourished on God's truth.
4. Godless myths and old wives' tales. God's truths.
5. To be godly.
6. Godliness.
7. The Living God— Savior of all people, Jesus Christ.
8. Not to regard age; Set an example for the believers in speech, conduct, love, faith, purity; Devote ourselves to public reading of Scripture (i.e. go to church); Preaching and teaching; Do not neglect your gifts.
9. It can discourage those who witnessed; Be diligent in the gifts and give ourselves wholly to them.
10. Save yourself and hearers.

Day 4
1. His face was radiant.
2. No.
3. He had spoken to the Lord.
4. They were afraid to come near him.
5. When he finished speaking to the Israelites.
6. When he spoke with the Lord.
7. Fear of the Lord. Various answers.
8. Death.
9. Righteousness.
10. Eternally.
11. Boldly.
12. Dull.
13. In Christ.
14. Heart.
15. Whenever anyone turns to the Lord.
16. Freedom.
17. Into His image with ever-increasing glory, which comes from the Lord, who is the Spirit.

Day 5
1. He made the city a heap of rubble, the fortified town a ruin.
2. Strong peoples will honor you, ruthless nations will revere you.
3. The poor.
4. He will swallow up death forever.
5. Surely this is our God we trusted in Him and He saved us. Let us rejoice and be glad in His salvation.

Day 1

1. That which was from the beginning— which we have seen with our eyes, which we have looked at and our hands have touched— this we proclaim concerning the Word of Life. The life appeared; we have seen it and testify to it, and we proclaim to you the eternal life which was with the Father and has appeared to us.
2. Not at all.
3. If we walk in light.
4. Follows God's commands— loving God above all else, loving others as yourself, walking in the fruits of the Spirit.
5. We have fellowship with one another and the blood of Jesus purifies us from all sin.
6. He is faithful and just and will forgive us our sins and purify us from all unrighteousness.

Day 2

1. The Holy Trinity— God, Jesus, and Holy Spirit.
2. In His own image; male and female.
3. God blessed them.
4. Be fruitful, fill the earth and subdue it, rule over the fish in the sea and birds in the sky and over every living creature that moves on the ground.
5. Every seed-bearing plant on the face of the whole earth and every tree that has fruit with seed in it. For food.
6. Yes!
7. It was very good.

Day 3

1. The everlasting God.
2. No.
3. He gives strength to the weary and increases the power of the weak.
4. They will renew their strength. They will soar on wings like eagles; they will run and not grow weary, they will walk and not be faint.

Day 4

1. Laodicea.
2. The Amen, The Faithful and True Witness, The Ruler of God's Creation.
3. Your deeds (of church in Laodicea); that you are neither cold nor hot.
4. Spit them out of His mouth.
5. I am rich, I have acquired wealth and do not need a thing.
6. They are wretched, pitiful, poor, blind, and naked.
7. To buy from Him gold refined in the fire (eternal, tried and true, perseverance) so you can become rich (eternal life through Jesus) and white clothes to wear (Jesus' purity and righteousness) salve on eyes. Repent and turn towards Him.
8. He rebukes and disciplines.
9. Be earnest and repent.
10. When you feel the prompting of Jesus through the Holy Spirit, obey, walk in the Spirit, accept Jesus as Lord (Romans 10:9) and you will walk in the eternal and abundant life Jesus gives.
11. The right to sit with Jesus on His throne.

Day 5

1. Various answers.
2. Various answers.
3. Various answers.
4. Various answers.

Notes

Notes

Notes

Made in the USA
Columbia, SC
07 February 2025

52724066R00080